FRONTIER FASCINATION

Adventures around the Swiss borders
on foot, by bicycle and kayak

by

Rupert Roschnik

Front cover picture from a photo by David Hefti. View of Piz Buin, 3312 m , in the Silvretta range, July 2nd, 2016

Main picture on the back cover by Euan Whittaker. View from the summit of the Pointe Dufour, 4632 m, in the Monte Rosa range, with the first climbers coming up the "voie normale", Gorner Glacier behind, July 15th, 2015.

Frontier Fascination

Copyright © (Rupert Roschnik 2019)

All rights reserved

No part of this book may be reproduced in any form by photocopying or any electronic or mechanical means, including information storage or retrieval systems, without permission in writing from both the copyright owner and the publisher of the book.

ISBN: 978-178456-678-4

Perfect Bound

First published 2019 by UPFRONT PUBLISHING
Peterborough, England.

An environmentally friendly book printed and bound in England by www.printondemand-worldwide.com

Contents

Foreword	1
From Basel to Lake Geneva	5
Cross-border commuters	27
From Lake Geneva to Ticino (the Valais)	29
Glacier shrinkage – personal experiences	56
Ticino and the Grisons part 1 (to Val Bregaglia)	58
Smuggling	79
The Grisons part 2 – from Val Bregaglia to Samnaun	83
The Grisons part 3 – from Samnaun to the Rhine	109
Mountain guides	124
The Upper Rhine, Lake Constance and Schaffhausen	126
From Schaffhausen to Basel	136

Appendices

    Information systems — 147
        Website
        Mobile phones, communication
        Geolocation

    Preparation and logistics — 149
        Planning
        Hiking and mountain equipment, bicycle
        Kayaks
        Navigation, orientation
        Physical training
        Logistics and accommodation

    Frontier stories – complete list and references — 152
    Daily log – itinerary and physical effort — 164
    List of summits and important Alpine cols — 178

Acknowledgements — 184

Foreword

It is June 4th 2015. I am sitting in my kayak on the Rhine in Kleinhüningen, a suburb just north of Basel next to the German border, ready to go. My intention is to follow the international boundary of Switzerland and return to this same place, but coming from the other direction. That would be 1935 km of frontier – walking, climbing, kayaking and bicycling. An ambitious project, an adventure that will undoubtedly be full of surprises. Will I succeed, how will it all turn out? Determined, I put the paddle in the water and I'm off, struggling upstream along the Rhine. One hour of that and I was already exhausted.

But let's go back to the beginning of the story . . .

Birth of a project

The idea for the project came to me in 1983 during a kayak course in Goumois on the Doubs river. I was 43 at the time. One day we paddled downstream from Goumois to St-Ursanne, mostly along the Franco-Swiss border. It was a beautiful day. I thought of other rivers on the Swiss border – the Versoix, the Inn and the Rhine. When I was younger I had read about some students who kayaked on the lakes of the Italian part of Switzerland in the 1930s. And there was also Lake Geneva, close to where we lived. One could perhaps connect all these bodies of water . . . And if we could also include the mountains, all these well-known summits, the 4000-metre peaks, and the interminable ridges connecting them! The idea was crazy, even completely insane. But it did not want to leave me, haunting me from time to time. Little by little, it became a project, a dream. Soon enough, I looked at topographic maps and some mountain guidebooks. The more

I studied them, the more I was impressed by the idea of the adventure. It was not impossible, even if difficult, indeed very difficult, to go around Switzerland along its borders, just using my arms and legs. Was such a project reasonable at the age of 75?

Who I am

I was born in 1940 in Vienna, Austria. After school in Vienna and England, I got a Ph.D. in chemistry in January 1965 at the University of Cambridge. After five years working in agriculture in Africa – in Southern Rhodesia (now Zimbabwe) and in Malawi – I settled with my family in Switzerland in 1970. I worked for Nestlé in the fields of laboratory and quality management until my retirement in 2004. My entire career took place in Vevey, with the exception of 2 years in a factory in Switzerland and 5 years divided between China and the United States. I have been married to Sally since 1965 and we have 3 children and 7 grandchildren. (Pictures of Sally on pages 40 and 119.)

I have always been passionate about mountains and geography. I've hiked, climbed and done ski touring since childhood and later took up kayaking. I consider myself a mountaineer rather than a rock climber and have completed many classic summits and difficult routes in the Alps. In Africa, I climbed Kilimanjaro and several peaks in Mount Kenya and the Ruwenzori.

Frontiers have always fascinated me, first and foremost the land borders, especially in Europe, having observed very early on that the language, the cuisine, the general atmosphere, the appearance and architecture of villages and towns, the practices of border guards and police, the currency (before the Euro) and much else changes the minute one crosses the border. Today you can travel more or less freely in Western Europe, but in my youth you needed visas everywhere!

Decision taken

Before putting my plan into practice, I had to first wait for my retirement. Sally and I had many other travel plans, so I had to wait. Moreover, at first I did not have the courage to tell her about my special project. Finally, it came out, almost in spite of me during a dinner with guests, who responded well – yes it is possible and a superb project! Luckily Sally understood that she could be part of it, that she was even indispensable for the logistics, and encouraged me! I began to plan seriously. Starting in Basel and going counter-clockwise, I could use the northwest of Switzerland and the Jura for warming up and getting into stride, and at the end take advantage of the current of the Rhine to descend by kayak from Sargans to Basel.

Physical map of Switzerland

The challenges

First of all there was the physical or athletic challenge. Technically, I felt up to it. I thought I could manage the alpine parts as well as the rivers. For safety, I needed companions, especially for some sections in the high mountains. One does not go alone on glaciers! Knowing no one who would be willing to go around with me, or even for just a few sections, I quickly decided to use professional mountain guides. Two other challenges: did I have the stamina and the tenacity needed?

Could I continue day after day, often under difficult weather conditions? It would be an enterprise lasting at least 3-4 months. Being a little stubborn, I was pretty confident about these points. We would see!

Then there was still the logistical challenge of having support, replacements for equipment, maps and supplies at strategic locations. Here my family was going to support me: Sally was ready to accompany me by car or public transport where necessary. Our son Roger lent me equipment and was always ready to help me out. There were other friends and former colleagues who offered their services and their time, but in practice it was impossible for me to give them specific appointments, because I often did not know where I was going to be in two or three days' time. There was one big exception: Peter Rowat, a former university colleague, a year younger than me, is a very keen mountaineer and hiker and has lived in the United States for many years. He was interested in my project and told me that he wanted to accompany me for 3-4 weeks, on any section. Wherever I was he would join me. This was fantastic!

Route-finding was another big challenge. I describe the solutions found later on. Another question: would I look for sponsors? I decided rapidly against it. I did not really want to beg, I did not want to be bound by contracts or other constraints on equipment, timing or advertising. I did not need the money, having set aside enough to pay any mountain guides. Daily expenses should not cost more than a "normal" holiday.

Circuits by other people

I should mention that I was not the first person to go round the Swiss frontiers, although I do claim to have thought of it independently, as well as being by far the eldest of them! To the best of my knowledge, two or three others have done the complete circuit. These are described in my website www.swiss-perimeter.ch together with some partial circuits.

But back to the Rhine in Basel!

From Basel to Lake Geneva

I'm off!

With Sally and grandson Neil watching anxiously, I headed first for the well-known monument at the Dreiländereck, a monument that symbolises the border point common to the three countries: Switzerland, France and Germany. It is on the Swiss side of the Rhine (but the real tripoint is 150 m away in the middle of the river).

I was shocked and dismayed on passing the Dreiländereck. The current was much stronger than I had expected and I had to go upstream against it for 2-3 km and then cross over to the other side to land near the Franco-Swiss border. Staying close to the bank I had less current, but I had to go outside a boat-restaurant anchored at the edge, which required much more effort for my arms. How long could I keep this up? After 1500 metres I had to cross to the other bank; needing more hard work to avoid losing too much ground because of the stronger current in the middle of the river, but I was soon close to the left bank near the border between Switzerland and France. However, there were huge construction sites on both sides of this border (Novartis Campus on the Swiss side) – high, vertical concrete walls had been built, making any landing impossible.

I had to go much further, under the Dreirosenbrücke, and at last arrived at some steps down to the river, near an old passenger ferry. Sally and grandson Neil were there to help me get the kayak out of the water and stow it on the roof of the car. I was already exhausted.

Construction work on the banks of the Rhine

No stopping! I took the bike for a stretch around the suburbs of Basel and Allschwil. A few miles further on, I left the bike to continue on foot.

The first metres on the bicycle

North of Allschwil, an interesting phenomenon: high class villas on the Swiss side, cultivated fields on the French side, right up to the garden fences, with hardly any space in between.

Neil had promised to accompany me for part of my trip and act as photographer. He was with me this first afternoon. At the Bänggenspitz we twice went through the narrowest part of Switzerland, 62 metres wide!

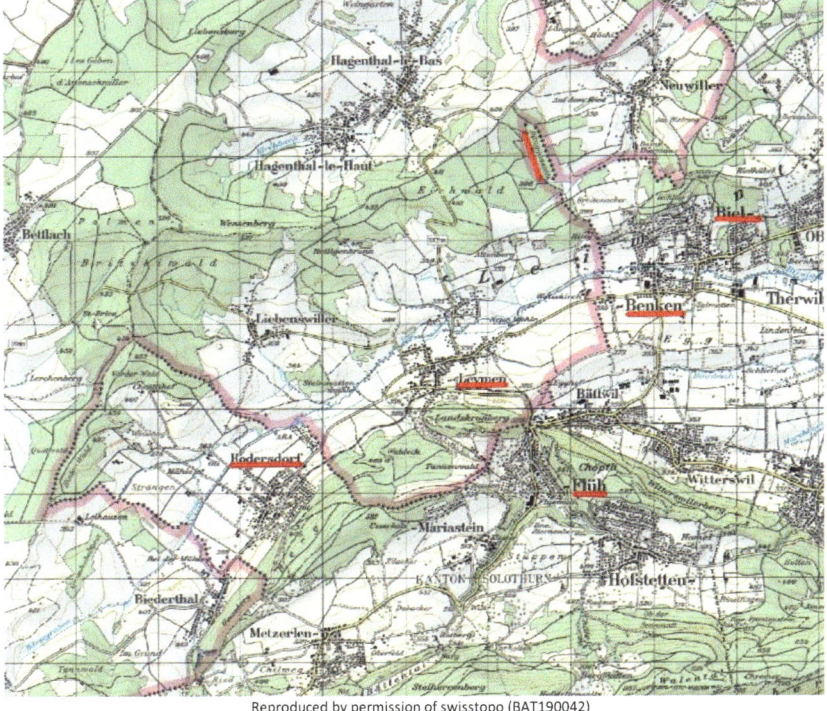

Reproduced by permission of swisstopo (BAT190042)

This part of the frontier in the forest to the north-west of Biel-Benken sticks out like a wedge into French territory. This odd configuration of the border in the Bänggenspitz was already documented in 1620. I believe that this strip of land was an ancient game reserve.

We at last arrived at Flüh, thirsty and quite tired. The day had been long. It was very hot weather and we had used up all our water. What a great first day of my journey! I was satisfied and happy. In about 7 hours I had progressed almost 30 km, kayaking, cycling and walking.

A huge beech tree

A friend from Basel, Christoph, wanted to accompany us on the second day. He arrived in Flüh in the famous tram no. 10 which connects Basel to Rodersdorf (canton Solothurn) through the village of Leymen in French territory. Christoph is fascinated by boundary markers and tried to photograph them all (!); so he was always a little behind Neil and me, trying to catch up with us. Route-finding was not too difficult and the boundary stones followed one another regularly. It was again very hot and fenced fields forced us to make some tedious detours. In the forest near Rodersdorf, we passed a huge beech tree, located about 5 metres inside the Swiss border. An information panel indicated that it was the largest beech tree in north-western Switzerland. We learned from this panel that compared to a normal beech tree ready to be logged, this impressive specimen had a three times larger trunk diameter and ten times more timber volume. It is about 40 m high and its timber volume was estimated at 35 m^3. During the 1st and 2nd World Wars, this beech saw "active service" as an observation post for the Swiss army. This service almost cost it its life. During World War II the inhabitants of Rodersdorf had to defend it against the German Wehrmacht who tried to cut it down.

Some beautiful forest trails took us to our first "summit", the Remelsberg, topped by a slender observation tower in concrete, just 832 m high and as such a very modest summit compared to what I would encounter later on.

The path that was no longer there

Further on, north of Miécourt, I had to make many detours because the whole border area there was very swampy and there were many obstacles – trees across the roads – certainly because of a recent severe storm. At one point, I took the only possible path marked on the map. But it didn't exist anymore! I followed its trace as best I could using the GPS and had to clamber between brambles, nettles, shrubs, trunks and branches of fallen trees on very muddy and swampy ground. In the end, I was exhausted. From the point of view of route finding, it was a good lesson; I learned to be wary of paths indicated on the map that were not marked in the field. Later I passed the "Borne des Trois Puissances" (Frontier stone of the Three Powers), the old tripoint between Switzerland, Germany and France between 1871 and 1918 (today between Switzerland, the department Haut-Rhin and the Territoire de Belfort). It was set up in September 1871 as a result of the peace treaty ending the Franco-German war of 1870-1871 which ceded Alsace and Lorraine to the German Empire.

Lonely landscapes

For 2-3 days, along the border around Porrentruy in the canton of Jura and along the Doubs, I saw almost nobody. The whole country seemed emptied of its inhabitants – there were large farms where I could hear machines humming and where I could see cattle but no humans, hamlets without a living soul, and closed customs buildings (I even saw one with a sign "for sale"!) It really felt like a forgotten corner of Switzerland!

A remote frontier stone

Brémoncourt

The Doubs and smugglers

Unlike other frontier rivers (the Rhine, the Rhone downstream from Geneva, the Inn downstream from Martina), for a section of 30 km downstream from Biaufond, the border along the Doubs does not run in the middle of the river but along its right bank. The river is therefore entirely French in this section and also the bridge at Goumois!

This peculiarity has a historical explanation: Louis XVI, perhaps keen on fishing, and the prince-bishop of Basel reached an agreement in 1780. By giving up his rights to the left bank of the river, the prince-bishop received 3 villages and other possessions on the right bank in exchange.

The Doubs gorge was also a hotbed of smuggling. An old smuggling path through the cliffs near Biaufond is well known under the name of "Les Echelles de la Mort" (the Ladders of Death). Today these are solid metal ladders and steps, but previously there were only tree trunks leaning against the cliffs, with notches for the feet. There is also an explanatory panel covering the subject along the Doubs. See special chapter on smuggling.

Back to civilisation

Between Goumois and Biaufond the trails and forest roads on the Swiss side of the Doubs are quite tedious – rising very high to avoid cliffs, and without any views because of the forest. From Biaufond on the other hand, the trail uses beautiful paths, often beside the river, with many bucolic places, and later, under high limestone cliffs, in quite wild scenery.

As I approached the famous waterfall Saut du Doubs and the restaurant at the end of the Lac des Brenets, the noise level increased. First because of groups of schoolchildren (we were close to the end of the school year), then because of hordes of retirees coming off the boats on the lake. This return to "civilisation" was deafening!

But soon I had complete peace paddling the 6 km to the other end of the lake. I landed and managed to pull the kayak up a grassy slope. The others were not there yet and there was nothing else to do except wait.

The Lac des Brenets

Later, Neil and I went up the valley of the Rançonnière, a small stream that acts as the frontier. After 2 km, the path decided to climb up over a cliff before coming down again, which seemed tedious, so we stayed in the creek bed in a gorge for some 500 metres. This turned out to be quite an adventure: very little water, but polluted and smelly, with mossy and very slippery stones, rocks, tree trunks and branches. Finally we reached the interesting border at Col des Roches, where we saw long queues of French commuter cars returning home at the end of the day.

The bed of the Rançonnière

The landscapes of the Jura

From the Col des Roches I climbed with Neil into the forest above and we suddenly found ourselves in another world: the "real" Jura, with its conifer-covered crests and long green valleys with farms and cows. And all these walls made of limestone blocks without mortar that mark the boundaries of the fields and the frontier.

It was also the first time that we had climbed above 1200 m in height. We hiked along miles and miles of trails that followed the wooded ridges and walls without mortar, more or less in a straight line, but with many small ups and downs. When the border made a right angle to pass from one crest to another, on the other hand, there were almost no trails in the right direction, only steep descents and climbs up through the undergrowth, often without a wall to mark the border. It was still quite hot and by the end of the day we felt humiliated when we had to beg for water at a farm.

Landscapes of the Jura

Once again on my own, I passed through the customs post of Les Verrières. This village is well known because the French East Army crossed the border here to take refuge in Switzerland in February 1871 – a historical event represented by the famous Bourbaki Panorama in Lucerne.

Another highlight for me was passing the France-Neuchâtel-Vaud tripoint near Ste-Croix. There are two boundary stones here – one marks the beginning of the Neuchâtel-Vaud border and the other the Franco-Swiss border. The latter one carries the date 1553 and must be the oldest border marker I saw during my tour of Switzerland.

Tripoint France-Vaud-Neuchâtel

Difficulties and obstacles

In the Jura, I had wet shoes and trousers every morning and often still in the afternoon if there was no sun. Why? If it had rained during the night, the long grass in the fields and the shrubs were wet, and after clear nights, the thick dew on the grass took over this task. In the forests, the roads and trails were often muddy or covered with puddles or impenetrable detritus left by foresters.

Three days after the Col des Roches, I was 70 km further on at the beginning of the Risoux forest ridge near Vallorbe. Thunderclaps announced an oncoming storm and heavy rain followed. I very soon had enough! I left the frontier and went down on a tarred forest road to a main road, where Sally was able to pick me up.

Completely lost!

June 15th was a very rainy day. I left well equipped against the weather and the wet vegetation and walked for long hours through the Risoux, without seeing anyone except a lady who was walking her dog (very far from any house – she must have entered the forest by car). Near the end, already on the part of the frontier that leads down to Bois d'Amont (F), I dropped my GPS onto the ground. It reacted badly by no longer displaying the Swiss topographic map but another "tourist" map that showed no trails. There was no way I could coax the right display back onto the screen.

In the Risoux

Without any sun to guide me, in the forest, on winding paths, with only a 1:50,000 scale map, I was soon lost. I followed signposts on the French side of the border, then a forest road that never stopped leading me uphill. I reached a viewpoint and could see down into the valley. But I did not recognise the place and later had to ask another solitary hiker where I was. How humiliating! But the hiker didn't have a map and didn't really know where he was either! But he did tell me he was coming from Bellefontaine and heading for Chapelle-des-Bois (both in France, the other side of the Risoux). Unbelievable! At one point I must have turned 90° to the right without realising it. Fortunately I had a signal for my mobile phone and could reach Sally. Explaining where I was was already more difficult ("I cannot find Bellefontaine on the road map"), but with the help of Neil as navigator she was able to rescue me an hour later. As for the GPS, luckily it worked perfectly again as soon as I changed the batteries!

Down to Lake Geneva

The next day, Sally dropped me near where I had crossed into France the day before. I immediately looked for the right path on the French side and after a few minutes passed a team of four foresters preparing tree trunks to be pulled out of the forest. Infernal noise of chain saws. A carpet of debris (which I had to cross) remained in the area and the path had been damaged by a large machine like a tractor. I was pretty disgusted but did not dare take any photos.

On the other side of the valley and the village of Bois d'Amont there is a rectangle of French territory, which includes forests on steep slopes and pastures further up. To understand this rectangle, we must first go back to the year 1802.

Napoleon wanted to build a (military) road between Les Rousses and the Geneva basin via the Col de la Faucille and simply exchanged the Dappes Valley against the Fricktal (canton Aargau) in 1802. In 1815, the Congress of Vienna returned this territory to Switzerland. But for years, the French continued to lay claim to this strategic road. In the end, in 1862, the Swiss Federal Council accepted an exchange of territories in this area. The rectangle above Bois d'Amont was left to France during this exchange formalised by the Treaty of Dappes in 1862, at the request of the local municipality in order to be able to keep 2-3 dairy farms in France and avoid paying customs duties on dairy products had these farms become Swiss.

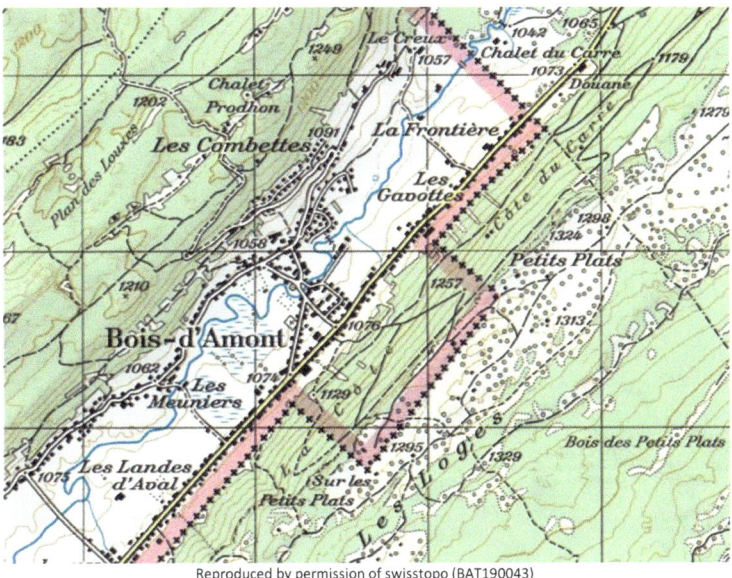
Frontier near Bois-d'Amont

In the pastures at the top I met an elderly lady, who drove a 4WD like a racing car, and who explained to me that there were still two dairies and some 200 cows up there on the French side.

Frontier stone at La Cure

After this there was a boring walk in wet grass to La Cure, where the border passes through the middle of the Franco-Swiss Hotel Arbez, which has two entrances, one from each country! Two hours later I had my first emotional view of Lake Geneva, a tangible sign that I arrived at the end of this part of the border and was approaching Geneva, and that I had therefore completed a good part of my journey!

An involuntary swim

The next incident took place on the Versoix River, which forms the Franco-Swiss border for 9 km. It's a classic for kayakers and I had done it more than once many years ago. The beginning is calm and very pleasant, but further down the Versoix begins to flow faster. My descent was made more difficult by the many tree trunks across the river. Then, after some 7 km, I was taken by surprise at a small waterfall and immediately capsized. The water was cold! I reached the bank quite easily – it was only 2-3 metres away and the water was not deep at this point. I recovered everything, drained the water from the boat and tried to get in touch with Sally and Neil – I had my GPS and my mobile phone in a waterproof bag. Soon enough, Neil came running on the trail along the bank and did the last 2 km in the kayak, while I went on foot. All's well that ends well!

Geneva airport

I still had to hike about 14 km on foot with Neil, through fields and commercial areas, along the barbed wire airport fence, to finally reach Meyrin. A day rich in incidents!

From Meyrin I cycled around a few CERN buildings and beyond. A stretch on foot through forests and some vineyards, followed by more cycling took me to the edge of the Rhone downstream from Geneva, from where I continued down the river in the kayak. After about 3 km, I found I could not land anywhere near a hydroelectric plant and its dam (fenced construction site), so I had to paddle upstream again some 500 m to find a suitable place to land. I continued on the mountain bike to reach the westernmost point of the Swiss border, and eventually reached the customs post at Perly, to the southwest of Geneva. I had to admit that I enjoyed cycling and this activity relieved my aching feet!

The Rhone at La Plaine

The westernmost point of Switzerland

The next day I was dropped in the same place with the bicycle and a sandwich, to do the rest of the southern Geneva border as far as Hermance on Lake Geneva. All went well, but I had to face a strong headwind once I had left the urban areas.

Lake Geneva

June 20th was the big day of the traverse of Lake Geneva. In single-seater kayak I would have needed 10-12 hours from Hermance to St-Gingolph, possibly even more. My other grandson Natan had told me a long time ago, as soon as he knew of my project, that he wanted to do Lake Geneva with me, in a two-seater kayak. An offer I could not refuse!

The conditions were ideal in the morning, no more wind and overcast, so not too hot, and sunny enough with a bit of wind in the afternoon. I was able to leave Hermance beach with Natan a little before 8 a.m. I now found I had a problem with my right shoulder, not being able to pull the paddle too hard, no doubt due to a bruise resulting from a fall in the forest about 10 days previously (I had tripped over a root hidden in long grass). The whole day was painful for me; luckily Natan (and Neil later on) are lads with big biceps. In fact they certainly did 75% of the work and without them I would never have succeeded in one day.

After paddling for 4 hours we were hailed from the shore a little beyond Thonon. It was Sally and Neil with our daughter Sonia (Natan and Neil's mother) on a small beach with a bar. They had speculated that we should be there at around midday.

So a longer break, a snack and a welcome rest. Natan and Neil agreed to change places for the rest of the stage.

At Hermance, with Sonia and Natan　　　　　　With Neil, after Thonon

It took us another 4 hours to reach at St-Gingolph, my shoulder ever more painful – I would grit my teeth and count 400 to 500 strokes before stopping to massage the shoulder, and then start the sequence again. Another short coffee stop in a village and we covered the last 5 km in record time. It was 6 p.m., it was sunny, we had done 50 km in a little less than 8 hours of paddling, and everyone was happy. I had succeeded in completing this stage in a single day!

We celebrated in a worthy manner and ate perch fillets on the menu of a creperie (!) on the French side of St-Gingolph. They came not from Lake Geneva but from Poland!

Arrival at St-Gingolph

There are indeed two St-Gingolph villages – one Swiss, the other French, only separated by a small stream. Looking from the other side of Lake Geneva, one sees only one built-up area. In the streets, coming from Switzerland, one immediately notices the difference between the two countries, especially as regards road signs and shops, newspaper kiosks and the distinctive red vertical rhombus showing tobacconists in France for example.

St-Gingolph is also known for its fire during the last war. On the morning of Sunday, July 23rd, 1944, German soldiers set fire to the French part of the village in retaliation for an attack by the Savoyard resistance the day before. A huge fire, clearly visible from the Swiss shore opposite, destroyed more than 80 houses mostly made of wood. More than 300 inhabitants of the French side took refuge on the Swiss side.

The church, shared by both communities, would be saved thanks to the intervention of Swiss Brigadier J. Schwarz who negotiated with the Germans. Also noteworthy was the activity of the German soldier Hartmann who, despite orders, crossed the border, seized a fire hose and sprinkled the church threatened by the flames, to protect it.

The next day, June 21st, a day of rest was essential, my first day of rest since leaving Basel: 16 days with 116 hours of sustained physical exercise, 550 km covered, for about 500 km of international border. Subsequently, the mountains of the Valais were waiting for me, with much more demanding and difficult stages, and other unexpected adventures, and perhaps surprises. Would I be able to keep going?

Cross-border commuters

In the course of my circuit I passed almost all the road crossings of the Swiss border. When it was morning or late afternoon, there was always steady or very heavy traffic, depending on the capacity of the road, and very often slowdowns or traffic jams. This phenomenon of traffic congestion is caused by cross-border commuters, mostly foreigners coming to work in Switzerland, and was most noticeable around the big cities (Basel, Geneva), but also in Le Locle, Biaufond, Vallorbe, La Cure, St. Margrethen and around Ticino and Schaffhausen, and even between Tirano (Italy) and the Val Poschiavo, significantly less at the Alpine passes of the Grand St-Bernard, Simplon (Gondo) and Splügen, for obvious reasons. I noticed that many minor road crossing points were being used by some cunning drivers around Geneva and along the Jura.

These cross-border workers are attracted by the generally higher salaries in Switzerland and are an essential component of the Swiss economy. But they must certainly also contribute to the economy of the regions beyond the border by providing income that is largely spent outside Switzerland. On the other hand, I can imagine that it would be quite difficult for entrepreneurs in a border region of France, for example, to set up a business or a factory because they could not pay their workforce at the same level as in Switzerland and because many well-trained workers would no longer be available.

Some statistics: the total number of foreign cross-border commuters is about 314,000, including 173,000 from France, 70,000 from Italy and 60,000 from Germany. There are a lot less coming from Austria. It is therefore not surprising that 117'000 cross the border nearly every day in the Lake Geneva region, 69'000 on the north-west border and 62'000 in Ticino. (Figures for the fourth quarter of 2018, rounded to nearest 1000). There are regional differences but the overall numbers have been increasing steadily in the past but declined slightly for the first time in 20 years during 2018.

26.3% of the active population in Switzerland is foreign; in Europe this rate is exceeded only by Luxembourg (over 50%).

There are also Swiss cross-border commuters who live abroad and work in Switzerland. There do not seem to be any precise statistics available on these; one estimate suggests almost 20'000 in the Geneva area. Of course, these only exacerbate the commuter traffic problems!

Official Swiss web sites:

https://www.bfs.admin.ch/bfs/fr/home.html

https://www.bfs.admin.ch/bfs/fr/home/statistiques/travail-remuneration/enquetes/staf.assetdetail.7427557.html

From Lake Geneva to Ticino

(The Valais)

Start in the mountains – it gets serious!

After the efforts on Lake Geneva and a well-deserved rest day, it was time to tackle the mountains and more serious things as regards altitude and Alpine terrain. The beginning was tough – a climb of 2100 metres in height from St-Gingolph to the summit of the Cornettes de Bise, partly on steep grass. This was also a thousand metres higher than the highest point reached in the Jura. In addition, my backpack was heavier than usual – Sally had prepared a huge picnic and I was carrying more water than I needed. The weather was acceptable, but very windy.

Taking it very slowly it took me six and a half hours to get to the top. There are always ibex up there – they know very well that they are protected in this region! – and I saw some of them. Sally later picked me up at a roadhead some 6-7 km further on, for another night at home.

Young ibex

The next day the weather was gloomy and rainy. It had been raining during the night, so the grass and bushes were all very wet. The paths were very muddy and slippery, so I had to be very careful. Just after the French ski lifts above Châtel (where big machines were at work to "improve" the ski slopes), it started raining again very hard just as I had to climb a steep slope of undergrowth and moss-covered stones to reach a small summit. I often had to pull myself up on roots and branches. Soon I was completely soaked and my boots full of water. Fortunately the rain stopped later and I could empty out my boots and wring the water out of my socks.

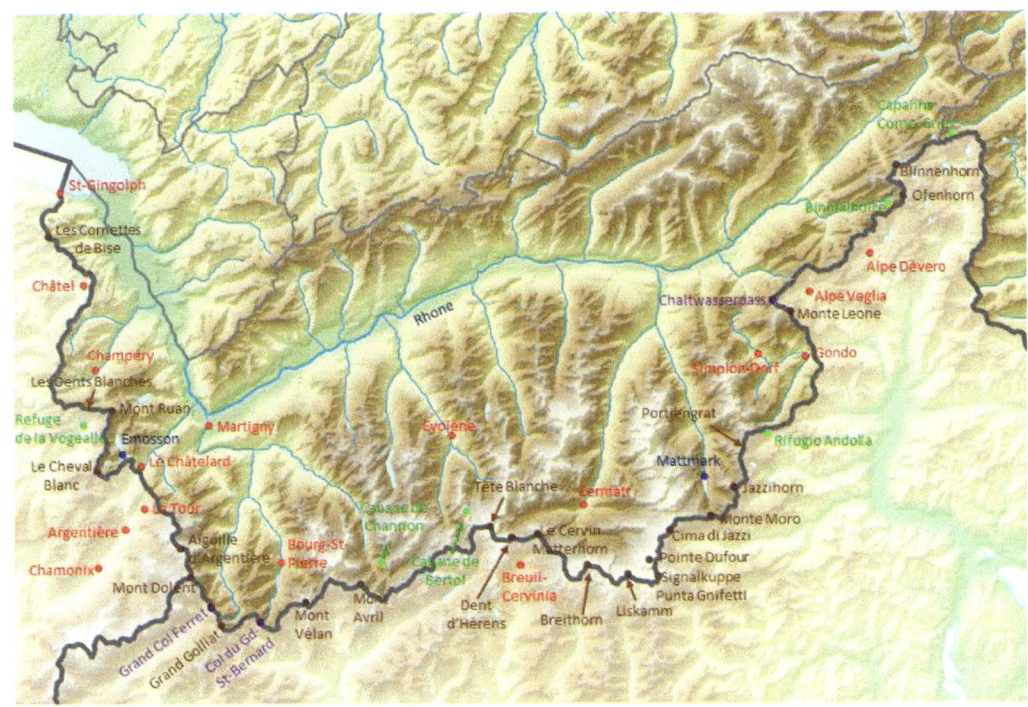

The Valais

My first mountain guide

The rest of the day passed without incident and I reached the day's destination, Alp Lapisa, a mountain dairy above Champéry, which offers accommodation and meals. Here I had arranged to meet my first guide, Victor, who would accompany me for the next three days. Victor Saunders is a well-known English mountaineer and guide living near Chamonix. He has climbed Everest 6 times, part of a very impressive record of achievements! So I was in good hands for the next section of the frontier, the traverse of the Dents Blanches.

Victor Saunders

Start in the Dents Blanches

Victor had done a reconnaissance a week previously with a colleague, trying the traverse in the opposite direction. However, they soon gave up because of the totally rotten and loose rock. Their conclusion: the complete traverse of the Dents Blanches would take far too much time and would probably be dangerous, if not impossible, under these conditions. Victor then convinced me not to attempt the complete traverse but to climb only the summits at each end, that is to say the Pointe de la Golette and the Dent de Barme, which are separated by 2 km of jagged ridges.

That's what we did: we left the mountain dairy at 5.00 a.m., heavy backpacks on our shoulders. We had planned at least one bivouac (without a sleeping bag!) and we probably carried too much food. The last rope lengths before the Pointe de la Golette, 2634 m, offered very pleasant rock climbing; then it was necessary to go down some 500 m on the French side before being able to climb up somewhat tediously on screes and snow slopes to the Dent de Barme, 2759 m. It was a beautiful day, with magnificent views. At the end we went down to the French Alpine Club Vogealle mountain hut. It was worth it: a comfortable dormitory and a good filling meal!

I was extremely happy! I had really enjoyed this day, the first "proper" day in the mountains, with a very early start and the first night in a mountain hut. It was also a day with considerable height differences – 2200 m uphill and 2090 m downhill, a record that would not be beaten until much later!

Waltz with crampons

After a nice breakfast in the hut at 3 a.m., we checked out at 4 a.m. A beautiful morning, but with clouds and cold wind on the ridges later in the day. There was more than 1100 m of uphill to the summit of Mont Ruan, 3044 m; the route-finding in the upper part was tricky and we had to retrace our steps once or twice, but we were well rewarded by a beautiful 360° view.

On top of Mont Ruan; Mont Blanc massif and Emosson lake behind

Mont Ruan gave me an excellent example of glacier shrinkage. I had climbed this summit with two friends in 1971! That year the route was quite easy – we crossed a small glacier below the summit to reach the southern ridge in a small chimney. 44 years later the glacier had lost about 20-30 metres in thickness, the chimney was almost inaccessible and we had to climb tricky screes and rock-covered ledges much further from the summit to get onto the ridge.

Later, following the frontier ridge to the south, the alternation of steep snowfields and scree meant that we were constantly putting on and taking off our crampons, at least a dozen times! We had intended to sleep in the open at a suitable col but the cold wind would have made this very uncomfortable in practice. So we then went down 600 m to a small shepherds' hut on the French side, where we found some thin mattresses, a sleeping bag and three blankets!

The next summit after the col had all its ledges so covered with snow that Victor did not want to attempt it. To go around it, we had to go down almost to the level of the Emosson lake, then go up a road to a restaurant below the wall of the Vieux Emosson dam, which had just been raised some 15 metres. Its reservoir was completely dry and the whole area a huge construction site. New tunnels had been dug all over the place. A new path, partly covered with soft snow, took us to the summit of the Cheval Blanc, 2831 m. More splendid views. Down again on the road, we learned that the road on top of the main wall of the Emosson dam was closed to pedestrians until 6 p.m., due to heavy construction site traffic. So we had to take a free shuttle bus organised for hikers. We were greeted at the other end of the dam by my son Roger and grandson Neil who took us down to the valley. Farewell to Victor, an excellent guide and companion for three days!

Into the Mont Blanc mountain range

After a day's rest at home, I was on my way again. It was nice and warm; in fact it was the beginning of a heat wave that lasted most of the summer. What a contrast to the awful summer of 2014! This beautiful weather helped my circuit enormously, but there were also disadvantages that I would encounter later.

From the Emosson dam, I went down to Le Châtelard, which marks the beginning of the Mont Blanc massif, after having lost time looking for the beginning of the trail because of the construction sites. At Le Châtelard customs post too, everything was fenced off around a nearby hydroelectric power station and the adjoining reservoirs, forcing me to make a lot of detours. The next landmark was the Col de Balme, which I reached partially on grassy ski slopes next to a ski lift. From this col I took a chairlift and a gondola to get down into the valley at Le Tour on the French side. In this way I could go up some thousand metres on these lifts the following day with the next guide, Graham, with all our equipment. A great saving in energy!

Sally was waiting for me at the valley station of the gondola in order to take me home. Unfortunately, when we returned home late that afternoon, she broke her left wrist against a tree in our garden while manoeuvring the car. I had to take her to the emergency clinic. In the end we learned that she had to go to the Lausanne hospital for surgery the next morning. This went well, but it was very tiresome for her because she could not drive for 3-4 weeks. But she insisted that I continue my tour without putting off the meeting with Graham the next day. I greatly appreciated her generosity, which allowed me to avoid further delays!

The second guide

Graham Frost is not only a professional guide but manages a guides' office in Evolène where he lives. It was he and his wife Janine who organised the guides for my 5 weeks in the Valais. Being themselves of Anglo-Saxon origin, they looked for guides among their contacts. All were English or Scottish but had lived for years in the Valais or the Chamonix region. They knew the area very well, in summer as well as in winter for ski touring.

Graham Frost

Graham had also invited an aspirant guide, Kenny, to join us for 2-3 days. We left the village of Le Tour by gondola and chairlift and a short walk took us up to the Col de Balme. It was getting late (the lifts only started at 9 a.m.), which would cost us dearly in the afternoon. The climb went well on the frontier ridge or on snow fields (snow already soft) on the Swiss side. We suffered a lot in the heat. The crux was a short climb up the Aiguille du Tour, 3540 m, competently led by Kenny. The following traverse of 2-3 km of the Plateau de Trient after 5 p.m., to reach the Trient hut, was almost unbearable because of the soft snow.

The next day we left before 4 a.m., to have good snow conditions. It had barely frozen during the short night. We crossed the Fenêtre de Saleinaz (very steep on the far side for 50 m), then crossed over to the Col du Chardonnet, whose ascent of about 120 m was very steep, a mixture of snow, ice and scree, and I was breathless at the end. From there, we had to go down a glacier for about 200 metres before attacking the last 800 metres up to the summit of the Aiguille d'Argentière. Now we were following the original route of Edward Whymper, who made the first ascent of this Aiguille in 1864 with Adams Reilly and three guides.

On the Aiguille d'Argentière

Delayed because of good weather!

The rapid softening of the snow prevented any attempt to traverse to other summits, so we descended by the normal route – quite steep at first – to the Refuge d'Argentière in France, where we had lunch and then a siesta. A sky without a single cloud, with excellent views in all directions, had made a day that filled me with joy.

We again started very early the next day to climb the Tour Noir. At 6 a.m. we were at the foot of a snowy couloir that led to the summit ridge. But it was too warm! Graham decided that it would be foolhardy to continue up this couloir, with real avalanche danger when coming down again maybe 3 hours later. So we said goodbye to the Tour Noir and went instead to the Col du Tour Noir, in just 20 minutes, before returning to the hut.

The next important summit was Mont Dolent, where Switzerland, France and Italy meet. In fact, the true tripoint is not quite at the summit, but 150 m to the northwest and 71 m lower where the North and West Ridges meet. The approach from the Argentière glacier was also compromised by the hot weather. The lower part of the climb up Mont Dolent would have involved difficult rock climbing and was exposed to falling rocks, while the steep snow slopes of the upper section would be extremely soft and dangerous by the time we reached them. So we decided to climb Mont Dolent from the south (Italian) side.

Argentière glacier, Mont Dolent behind

So down from the hut to the village of Argentière in the Chamonix valley, where we found heat wave conditions. We all went home and Graham arranged to meet me in the Swiss Val Ferret the next morning.

Soft snow on Mont Dolent

It was again a beautiful sunny day. Graham drove his 4WD to an agritourism alp called La Peule. After a snack there, we went up to the frontier at Grand Col Ferret. This section is part of the Tour du Mont Blanc and we met a large number of hikers of different nationalities who were doing this tour, also a number of mountain bikers. Then we went across to the Petit Col Ferret and up to the Italian Cesare Fiorio bivouac shelter, at 2729 m, to spend a quiet afternoon before climbing Mont Dolent. Early bed.

Cesare Fiorio bivouac shelter, Mont Dolent on left behind

It was an even earlier start – wake up at 2 a.m., leave at 2.30. An hour's climb on bands of smooth rock interspersed with snowfields, took us to the glacier. From there, we had an exhausting climb, often steep or very steep, in rotten and soft snow – it had not frozen during the night! – in which Graham had to make the tracks. The sky was slightly overcast, so we were not too exposed to the sun. Finally, we were at the top at 6.30. Beautiful panoramas in all directions. The descent was just as exhausting for me, especially the slope just under the summit, very steep and with a slightly crusted snow surface. For me, this summit marked the end of the Swiss border with France and I was very happy to have completed this section. And as for Mont Dolent, a big thank you to Graham Frost!

Over the Grand-St-Bernard Pass

For the next stage I had three companions, grandson Neil, son Roger and a good friend, Yves Stettler, who had done the famous Glacier Patrol with Roger at least three times. The next major summit on the frontier was the Grand Golliat. With 4 of us, the northwest ridge from Grand Col Ferret seemed too long. So I decided to take the "voie normale" from the Grand-St-Bernard road, on the Italian side. At the very top, there was too much snow on a rock barrier, so we opted to go up the east face which had no snow on it and reached a point just below the east summit.

While trying to glissade on snow that was too hard for his shoes, Neil reached the scree below too fast, fell and ended up with some cuts on his legs. Bleeding and a little shocked, he was escorted to the car by Roger, while Yves and I traversed the entire frontier ridge to the Grand-St-Bernard Pass. Just before the pass, we were greeted by Sally, our younger daughter Natalie and her three children. It was a Saturday and it was sunny – there were a lot of people at the pass, crowds of tourists, cars and noisy motorbikes . . .

At the Col du Grand-St-Bernard
Sally, Inès, myself, Yves Stettler, Neil, Roger, Tessa

I had arranged to meet Dave Green, the new guide for the next 8 days, at the parking lot at the Swiss entrance of the Grand-St-Bernard road tunnel, at 6 a.m. the next morning. To do this I had to leave home already at half-past four. Having posted blogs the evening before up to midnight and even later, I found myself struggling against sleep – on the monotonous and empty motorway, I was in real danger of falling asleep! Open windows, music, singing, and other tricks not to nod off. I stopped at a petrol station hoping for a coffee, but it was closed. I had to settle for a Coke bought from a vending machine. Once past Martigny, I had a more winding road and there was less danger, but I was always a little afraid of losing my concentration.

Dave was already waiting for me. He had spent the night in his van. We organised ourselves quickly as regards gear and food and immediately started on the climb up to the Col d'Annibal, well known to ski mountaineers. It started with more than 1000 metres uphill on grass, scree and moraines, all of them steep, which took us almost 4 hours. Then the Hannibal Ridge itself was almost as bad, with many unstable rocks and scree. Not to be recommended! On reaching the summit of Mont Vélan, we found many tracks in the soft snow which led us down to the Vélan Hut by the normal route. We arrived there just in time for supper; I had been able to call earlier from a small col, which was trickier and longer than the last time I did it 20 years ago or more, because of the shrinkage of the glaciers on both sides. We were the only visitors in the hut that night. The day before (a Saturday) there had been 25 and all of them reached the summit.

Stuck – it's still too warm!

When I talked to Dave about the next day and how to get to the Chanrion Hut, his response upset me! "The Col du Sonadon is not possible, the Plateau du Couloir before this pass is too dangerous". He described how there are accidents there every year because of falling rocks and that he himself had witnessed a fatal accident two years ago. In a "normal" year he would do it only at 5 o'clock in the morning after a freezing night, but this year it is not freezing at night, it's too dangerous, that's all!

I was very disappointed, especially since it left me the entire responsibility to organise the next steps. The only reasonable way out was to go down to Bourg-St-Pierre and use road transport. So I contacted Yves Stettler who kindly picked us up above this village and took us to the next valley where he had organised a taxi to get us past the Mauvoisin dam and lake. This road is allowed only for taxis and takes about an hour. I had still hoped to hike up to the frontier and possibly climb Mont Avril in the afternoon. However, the taxi dropped us off at the Chanrion Hut at around 1 p.m. and supper was announced for 6.30 p.m. There was not enough time for this trip under good conditions. A bad day for the frontier!

The next day we reached a bivouac hut close to the frontier, climbing along ledges full of scree and up steep snow slopes. In the afternoon, we crossed a small glacier to reach the Col d'Otemma. The snow was very soft and we could not do either of the neighbouring peaks. We were alone at the very comfortable bivouac shelter; the views were superb; there was a storm during the night, with a lot of lightning, thunder and rain.

Col d'Otemma

Detours and delays

More unwelcome surprises: Dave informed me that some other sections are "out of bounds" because dangerous or too long / difficult or impossible, either because of his own knowledge, or after discussion with Graham Frost or with other guides. These sections included the Col du Mont Brulé (which surprised me the most because I had done it more than once on skis – "Ah, but in summer it's different!") and the long east ridge of the Dent d'Hérens. My options were then quite limited. In particular, it was necessary to leave out the Dent d'Hérens, which had to be climbed from a hut on the Italian side, itself only accessible from the Col de Valpelline, with a return by the same route, at a cost of at least 2 additional days. These two days were not acceptable at this time because of a deadline at the Matterhorn: the Swiss authorities had decided to close their side of the mountain already a couple of days before the 150th anniversary of the first ascent by Whymper, companions and guides on July 14th, 1865. They were afraid that too many climbers would attempt the summit on that day to "celebrate" the anniversary. The Italians were expected to follow suit by also closing their side of the mountain. And we had already decided with Graham Frost to climb the Matterhorn from the Italian side because there would be too many people on the normal Hörnli ridge on the Swiss side, even without the anniversary.

A pity about the Dent d'Hérens because it would have been the first 4000-metre summit of my circuit. But I reminded myself that I had already climbed this summit in 1964! On the other hand, the caution of the guides was quite understandable. It was much too warm, nothing froze during the night, the snow was still soft, progress was slow, there was a danger of falling rocks, and it was impossible to do anything serious in the afternoons.

So we continued to the Bertol Hut. The following day, we climbed up to the Tête Blanche with other groups doing the Haute Route from Chamonix to Zermatt. It had – for the first time in over a week – frozen during the night and walking with crampons was a real pleasure. So much so that we continued without stopping and we were soon in the moraines of the Zmutt Glacier. These moraines were tedious but we emerged at the end and took paths leading to Zmutt and Zermatt, both of us with sore feet. Dave took the train to Martigny to pick up his van from the entrance to the Grand-St-Bernard road tunnel, while I spent a nice afternoon and evening with Sally and Neil who had come up by train.

July 10th was earmarked for arriving at the Rifugio Duca degli Abruzzi (or Rifugio Oriondé) above Cervinia village, the starting point for the Lion Ridge on the Matterhorn. Dave and I took the cable car to the Klein Matterhorn (now called "Glacier Paradise"!); we walked down to the frontier at Testa Grigia and took other cable cars down to Plan Maison, above Cervinia. From there we climbed up to the hut. There, another surprise: Dave found that he had a problem in one foot, probably the result of the descent to Zermatt two days ago, and could not do the Matterhorn with me. He started phoning Graham Frost to find a replacement guide. Not wanting to waste time, I asked for the help of the hut warden, who referred me to the Bureau des Guides in Cervinia. It was already almost 6 p.m. and a lady told me she was going to try to find someone who was ready to climb the very next day, going up and down the same day. Finally, around 7 p.m., she announced that she had found somebody but I had to call him to confirm. This I quickly did and Giorgio Cazzanelli, as he was called, fixed to meet at the hut in order to leave at 3:30 a.m.! You can imagine how happy and relieved I was!

The Rifugio Oriondé is very nice, but we had to sleep on mattresses on the floor because we had not booked ahead and there were no more beds.

The Matterhorn adventure

Giorgio arrived by motorcycle before three o'clock; I heard him and got up to quickly have a cup of coffee with him. Then we started in the dark. He spoke French well and was excellent. About 45 years old, he knew every metre of the way, every shortcut, every piton. We made good progress and reached the top at 10:15, after half an hour at the Carrel Hut for a cup or two of tea. The whole climb was exhilarating. There are many fixed ropes along the way where you have to pull yourself up with your arms, which I found quite tiring. It was fine, but with a strong cold wind on the ridges. And a continuous ballet of helicopters buzzing around the mountain, full of rich tourists anxious for good aerial photos of this famous icon of the Swiss Alps.

The Matterhorn (from the Dent d'Hérens)   Giorgio Cazzanelli

Going down again we took about the same time since Giorgio was more cautious, or more tired? At the fixed ropes, he lowered me down on his rope like a sack of flour – except that I had to stay fairly horizontal, "walk" down backwards and put my feet in the right place. This way saved time and was easier for me. Again, Giorgio's knowledge of the route impressed me. Once, before lowering me down, he said: "You see that snowy ledge down there where you'll end up? Just go about 2 metres to the right and clip into the piton you'll find there." And the peg was exactly where he said it was! The whole round trip was a unique and wonderful experience! I have often been asked which was my best day in the whole border circuit. It is difficult to pinpoint a specific day; there were many fantastic days, but the ascent of the Matterhorn with Giorgio was certainly a highlight.

Meanwhile, Dave had to hang out all day at the hut. The next day we returned to Klein Matterhorn, but not before I had gone down to Cervinia where I found the Bureau des Guides, paid for Giorgio and thanked the lady for her efforts to have found me an excellent guide.

A new guide, Euan Whittaker, arrived at midday to take the place of Dave who left for Zermatt and beyond to have his foot examined properly. With Euan I climbed slowly up the Breithorn, following a track well worn by dozens of other mountaineers, mainly Italians. It was a Sunday and I reckoned there were at least 200 people on the summit that day! Euan, what a contrast to Dave! He was younger, very enthusiastic and had a small camera that he frequently took out to take pictures. We spent the night at the Klein Matterhorn dormitory: no warden, expensive, but well organised, with all facilities.

Terrible twins and a pleasant encounter

On July 13th we left at 4 a.m. There was good hard snow, also gusts of wind, but we were often sheltered on the Italian side. We reached the top of Pollux by its southwest ridge, with 3 fixed ropes, then the top of Castor, and the Rifugio Quintino Sella at 11 o'clock. It was too cold to stop. I wrote the following in my blog of the day:

They did not want us to come, so threw some bad weather at us, in the form of a very strong, cold north wind that nearly blew us off their summit ridges. First Pollux, then Castor, most impolite!

Fixed rope on SW ridge; notice the crampons scraping the rock!

Pollux, the summit ridge

Behind the counter at the hut I saw a girl who seemed familiar to me. I immediately thought. "Where have I seen her before?" But she recognized me first. It was Federica (Feddy) Garofalo, who had rented a room in my daughter Sonia's house in Cambridge for a few months a year ago. I had met her and learned that she liked mountains and spent the summer working at a mountain hut, which was quite close to her home in the Valle d'Aosta. She had an advantage over me though – she knew I was going around the Swiss border and she also knew from my blogs that I was in the area!

The next summit should have been the Liskamm but other guides and the hut warden had all told us that no one had yet made the critical traverse of the knife-edge ridge this year; moreover, there was still a strong north wind on the ridges. We had to go around this summit, crossing the Naso, a snowy spur south of Liskamm, with a steep icy slope to overcome it. We were the first ones that day and Euan did a good job here, with three rope lengths of 60 metres with belays on ice screws.

The highest mountain hut in the Alps

The rest of the day was simply a laborious walk on snowfields. There were beautiful snow ridges on top of the first two summits, the Ludwigshöhe and the Parrotspitze. At last we arrived at the third 4000-metre peak of the day, the Signalkuppe or Punta Gnifetti, 4554 m, on which is perched the Italian hut Regina Margherita, the highest mountain hut in the Alps. We had good weather all day, with a lot of wind on all the ridges. An itinerary largely on good hard snow, crampons worn all along, from hut to hut, the same as the day before.

At the hut we met another guide and his client, who had just traversed the Liskamm! When I asked if there was not a lot of wind, the guide replied, "Yes, but it was a constant wind, there were no gusts." Despite this slight disappointment, I was very happy with the trek made that day. The meal here was probably the best I had among all the mountain huts visited – steak and chips, and chocolate pie as a dessert!

Regina Margherita mountain hut

Evening at the Signalkuppe / Punta Gnifetti

The next day became another highlight of my mountain circuit because we were able to climb the highest mountain in Switzerland, the Pointe Dufour (or Dufourspitze, 4634 m) in the Monte Rosa range. It lies about 300 m inside the Swiss border and is named after Guillaume-Henri Dufour, Swiss engineer, general and statesman, also co-founder of the Red Cross, who was responsible for issuing the first topographic map of the whole of Switzerland based on precise measurements.

Euan and I left early for the Zumsteinspitze. The sky was clear, the wind was cold. We witnessed a beautiful sunrise from this summit 20 minutes later. The snowy ridge connecting it to the Pointe Dufour was a real knife-edge, the narrowest I've ever seen, some 200 metres requiring the skills of a tightrope walker. I only fixed my gaze at the next step without looking at the abyss on either side!

Between Zumsteinspitze and Pointe Dufour

Euan Whittaker

A helicopter rescue seen close up

There followed very pleasant climbing on good rock, with some patches of snow. Halfway along, we witnessed a rescue operation first-hand. We had noticed a group of climbers to our right and had wondered why they were not moving.

Suddenly at about 7 a.m. a red Air Zermatt helicopter came and hovered over us; it disappeared but returned a few moments later with a doctor / mountaineer hanging on the end of a long rope. He was deposited next to the group of three mountaineers within 30 metres of us. Then two of the climbers were tied to the big hook at the end of the rope and were lifted off and away. A few minutes later, the helicopter came back and picked up the doctor and an injured girl, on some sort of stretcher. Amazing precision! We learned later that the climbers had needed to wait all night for their rescue.

More pleasant climbing on snow and rock brought us past the Grenzgipfel and the Pointe Dunant (which we hardly noticed) to the top of the Pointe Dufour. We were the first at the top that day – the first climbers coming from the other side by the normal route arrived a few minutes later. Then we went down some fixed ropes to the "Silbersattel" and climbed our fifth 4000 m summit of the day, the Nordend, which is the last of the high mountains of the Monte Rosa massif.

View from the Pointe Dufour

Euan did not want to go down the famous Santa Caterina ridge, a very difficult rock climb, so we went down to the Monte Rosa Hut. It was a long way down, passing interesting seracs and crevasses, to reach the new hut with its striking shape and modern amenities.

The next day we had planned to go in the direction of Monte Moro. It was sunny all day. We crossed moraines, polished rocks and streams under the Monte Rosa Glacier to reach the bare ice of the upper Gorner Glacier. Going up it, we were soon on snow, but the surface was hard, there were only a few crevasses and we made good progress to the summit of the Cima di Jazzi, 3803 m, a very beautiful belvedere.

Crevasses and soft snow

We wanted to reach at least a bivouac-shelter only 2-3 km further on but the snow was very soft on this side, exposed to the sun. In addition, gaping crevasses crossed the entire glacier. Even if we had found snow bridges to cross them, we could hardly trust them: the risk of one collapsing was already too great (at midday!). Hence the wise and disappointing decision to turn back and make for the Gornergrat to descend to Zermatt and a rest day.

In the afternoon of July 18th I met my fifth guide, Dave Kenyon. We drove up to the Mattmark dam and from there hiked up to the Monte Moro Pass and a mountain hut just on the Italian side. We started in cloudy weather, but an hour later it started to rain, not very hard, but continuously and there was thunder in the air. At 7 p.m. we reached the pass and 15 minutes later we were removing our wet clothes in the hut. The welcome was warm and we had a good meal. The "lobby" of the dormitories had a large pellet stove that was burning all night long. Initially, it showed 19°C, but the next morning the temperature was stifling at 28°C; this was good for drying out shoes and clothes, but otherwise unbearable.

From this hut we climbed 3-4 summits along the border ridge. There was no path at all; most of the time we were going through scree, stony rubble and tiresome unstable boulder fields, and we realised that we were not moving as fast as we expected on this type of terrain. The next summit, the Jazzihorn and the subsequent descent to the next pass cost us a lot of time. Clouds were threatening and we decided to aim for the Camposecco Italian bivouac-hut via a small col of the same name.

Dave Kenyon, Monte Rosa massif behind

Race against time

This col is a rather steep-sided cleft and a little hidden; we went too far and climbed the next shoulder. The GPS told me that we needed to go down to the bottom of the small valley leading to the pass, but Dave thought it would be better to climb to the top of the shoulder and descend to the pass on the ridge. This descent of only 50 m in height was classified "easy" in our guide but we did not find the right way. We had to rope up and do some tricky climbing while it started to drizzle and a thunderstorm was raging on the other side of the valley. We hurried to arrive at the bivouac after 13 hours of hiking, without stops. I had to borrow matches from an employee of the nearby hydroelectric facility (and I also got two beers off him) and we brewed tea and ate the little food we had.

After a comfortable night (mattresses and blankets in the hut) we went towards the Rifugio Andolla that we should have reached the day before. We took almost 4 hours to get there but we were able to avoid the difficult Portjengrat, which was necessary because all the guides had advised against it and the subsequent ridge. A late breakfast at the hut, then the climb up to the Andolla Pass, followed by the long descent to the border village of Gondo, which I had promised to reach that day (meeting with Sally who came by train, and a booking at Simplon Dorf).

The Gondo disaster

It happened on October 14th, 2000. A landslide caused by heavy rains washed away part of the village, severely damaging the Stockalper Tower and killing 13 people, about 10 percent of the population. This tragedy created a surge of solidarity that had never been seen before, since 700,000 Swiss gave a donation for the reconstruction of the village. The Stockalper Tower, originally built by the powerful family of Upper Valais traders, was repaired and reopened in 2007.

Following the Gondo border to the summit of Monte Leone would have involved a climb of 2750 vertical metres, and even more if all the intermediate cols and peaks were counted. Moreover, the first section consists of very steep rubble and scree, normally done in descent and by abseiling. Dave and I decided it was too much, especially with heavy backpacks! So we opted for a departure from the Simplon hospice, which saved us 1200 m climbing. But because we could only have breakfast at 7 a.m. at the hotel in Simplon Dorf we left quite late. We made good progress but suffered from the heat and soft snow later. The easy climbing on large slabs and blocks on the final ridge seemed endless but we were at the top around 2 p.m.

The weather was reasonable, but with a lot of clouds. During the descent, Dave proposed to cross directly to the Monte Leone Hut, without losing height, but we were blocked by ravines and small cliffs and had to go down anyway – the result was a waste of time, at least 30 minutes. Moral: beware of shortcuts in the mountains!

Shrinkage of a glacier - scree and unstable rock

The next day, already July 22nd, it was very foggy in the morning and the forecast was not good. However, we did the Wasenhorn, a fairly easy climb, mainly on scree with traces of paths. From the top, we could see the valley briefly through the clouds.

Continuing on the border ridge not being advisable under these conditions, we went on to Alpe Veglia in Italy. Some 400 m after the Chaltwasserpass there was a steep and delicate descent on a few short cliffs exposed by the shrinking of the glacier, with several metal chains and footrests. Then, after the remaining snowfields of a small glacier and moraines the path became more pleasant and led us to Alpe Veglia. Halfway it started to rain, enough to make us put on rain gear, but not enough to soak us. It only lasted half an hour and when we arrived at the Rifugio Città d'Arona around midday, we were already dry and there was even some sun.

Halfway there too, without knowing it, we were about 1550 metres above the Simplon railway tunnel. And about 700 m northwest and 660 m higher on the ridge, where the tunnel underneath passes across the border, 100 m from a summit called Tunnelspitz, is a boundary stone, number 3. Incidentally, the construction of the first Simplon tunnel between 1898 and 1905 was heroic because the hydraulic drills were still rudimentary. The working conditions for the workers were very difficult – more than 45°C inside the tunnel! – 106 workers left their lives in the tunnel and there were several strikes. The opening of the tunnel in 1906 allowed a gain of 13 hours travel time on the distance Lausanne-Milan!

Frontier marker near the Tunnelspitz

The next day, the forecasts were still not very good and we were a bit stuck on the Italian side of the border. So we had a fairly long day to get to the Binntal hut. The trails were well signposted and gave us no problems, apart from a steep, stony and vicious section where a climb of 330 m cost us a good 45 minutes. We treated ourselves to an ice cream at Alpe Dèvero and went on to the next hamlet for a spaghetti dish as a midday meal. Finally, we reached the Binntal Hut just inside Switzerland. It was partly covered all day, with a few drops of rain.

Mission: impossible?

We had committed to reach the Corno-Gries Hut the next day. Dave had to go home the day after and I had arranged to meet Peter Rowat, a former mountaineer friend, who would be there that night and would accompany me for the next 3-4 weeks. When I mentioned Corno-Gries to the warden of the Binntal Hut, a nice lady, she started saying that this was impossible, but corrected herself and said it would be very difficult and time consuming. I did not dare tell her that we also intended to take in three summits!

So we left at 6 a.m. for the summit of the Ofenhorn. It was foggy all day, which did not help our route-finding. Another problem was that the glaciers had receded, leaving many exposed rock outcrops that were marked neither on our maps and nor on the GPS. This was very visible below the summit of the Ofenhorn when traversing to the next col. Later, we had planned to traverse on snow slopes below a rocky ridge, but Dave figured we could traverse across it to avoid losing height. In practice, this ridge – unnamed on the map and barely mentioned in the guide – gave interesting climbing, but the many gendarmes in the form of huge blocks of rock cost us a lot of time. I felt that this exercise cost us up to an hour of valuable time.

Crossing the next summit was easy, as was the descent down the upper part of the Hohsand Glacier with its crevasses. We then traversed the entire southern face of the Blinnenhorn, below its south-west ridge, on scree and snowfields, to reach the top of a small residual glacier. Three rope lengths on steep scree, where everything we touched collapsed and slid down, allowed us to reach the ridge. How Dave managed to lead those lengths I will never understand! However, we were on the summit of the Blinnenhorn around 16h30, from where I managed to call the warden of the Capanna Corno-Gries; she was not too happy about our late arrival.

We finally arrived at the hut at 8 p.m. after crossing the Gries Glacier in the fog, and were greeted by Peter (and his wife Nona) who had persuaded the warden to keep supper for us. In fact Peter had come a little way to meet us and the meeting, after some 15 years without having seen each other, took place some 400 metres before the hut. I was very happy to see him! To complete the itinerary of that day, a distance of 25 km with more than 2000 m of climbing and descent, we had put in 14 hours, almost without stopping! The Corno-Gries Hut lies 2-3 km inside the canton of Ticino, so this stage marked the end of the Valais-Italy border.

Glacier shrinkage, personal experiences

I noticed clear examples of glacier shrinkage or recession in more than one place.

The first example was near the summit of Mont Ruan. This is described in the previous chapter (page 32).

There were two other places where glacier shrinkage had turned a fairly easy descent on a snow and ice slope into something quite tricky and delicate. Below the Camposecco col this gave us difficult route-finding to weave our way down polished slabs before we could safely set foot on a residual glacier. Then, about 400 metres after the Chaltwasserpass the marked trail led down a few short steep cliffs, with several metal chains, handholds and footrests.

Another example was on the Ofenhorn, at the end of the Binntal. I had been up this summit 2-3 times on skis many years ago, climbing the snow slopes of its east face. In 2015 we climbed from the south via the Eggerscharte and Arbola Glacier. There is not much left of this glacier – we were climbing snow-covered couloirs and rocks. But it was when we reached the summit that the changes were most noticeable. The summit itself was entirely rocky, not covered in snow. However, it was the east face that had changed quite dramatically. The whole slope was now divided into two or three parts by tongues of rock from the summit downwards, with bare ice and some crevasses in between. Further down, the traverse to the next col (Hohsandjoch) was done partly on rock bands and outcrops (which were marked neither on my maps nor on the GPS, supposedly updated within the last few years.)

The glacier at the end of the 1970s   And what is left today!

The Gries glacier which we went down later the same day is another good example of global warming. In the 1970s, the glacier front reached far enough to calve into the reservoir created by the construction of the dam in 1965. One could even see some icebergs (albeit of very modest size) floating in the lake below the Gries border pass. 40 years later, no more ice in the lake. What remains of the glacier has receded into the mountains.

I also had the opportunity to compare the appearance of the north face of the Dent d'Hérens with a photo I had taken in 1964. It can be seen that the ice cliffs are quite similar, while the snow has disappeared from other slopes.

1964-07-24

2015-07-09

Ticino and the Grisons, first part

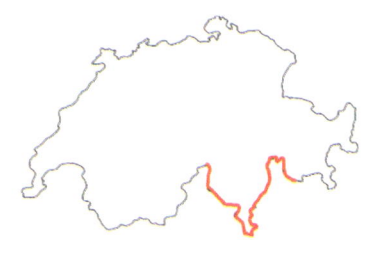

I left the Corno-Gries Hut with Peter, who was to be my companion for the next 3 weeks. His wife Nona not only ensured the logistics, that is to say the moving of the car, but joined us almost every night in a mountain hut (by hiking up on foot) or in another accommodation.

Peter comes from Scotland. He is a long-time mountain companion. We were in the same mountaineering club at university, we both participated in an expedition to the Stauning Alps in East Greenland in 1963 and we set up our own mini-expedition to Alaska in 1976. He lives in La Jolla, California and is still a very active hiker, both in summer and winter, especially in North America. Nona, of American origin, is a doctor (paediatrics) and specialises in hiking long trails in the United States, having done the Appalachian Trail and the Continental Divide Trail among others.

It was really wonderful to have them with me, as I didn't have to worry about meeting-places and timing!

Frontier marker and signs at the Bocchetta di Val Maggia

We quickly reached the Passo San Giacomo and the Bocchetta di Val Maggia on marked paths. The sun was shining, another superb day! A bit later, we put on crampons to climb the Basòdino Glacier. I had done this route on skis twice some years ago. There is a rocky barrier halfway up that you could ski down easily on a snow-covered ramp. Today, the glacier is much less bulky and it was necessary to climb ten metres on rocks. I was in front and Peter was following me more and more slowly – he was lacking altitude training and he was suffering above about 2600 m. And it was his first day of serious hiking!

The descent from the top of the Basòdino along its SSW ridge proved to be exhilarating – sections of knife-edge ridge on good rock. On reaching the next col, we found a metal ring indicating an abseil point. Two abseils took us down to snowfields, steep at first, pleasant afterwards. We soon found footpaths, cairns and finally red and white marks, which led us to the friendly Rifugio Piano delle Creste, where we were welcomed even arriving without a reservation at supper time, after more than 10 hours of hiking.

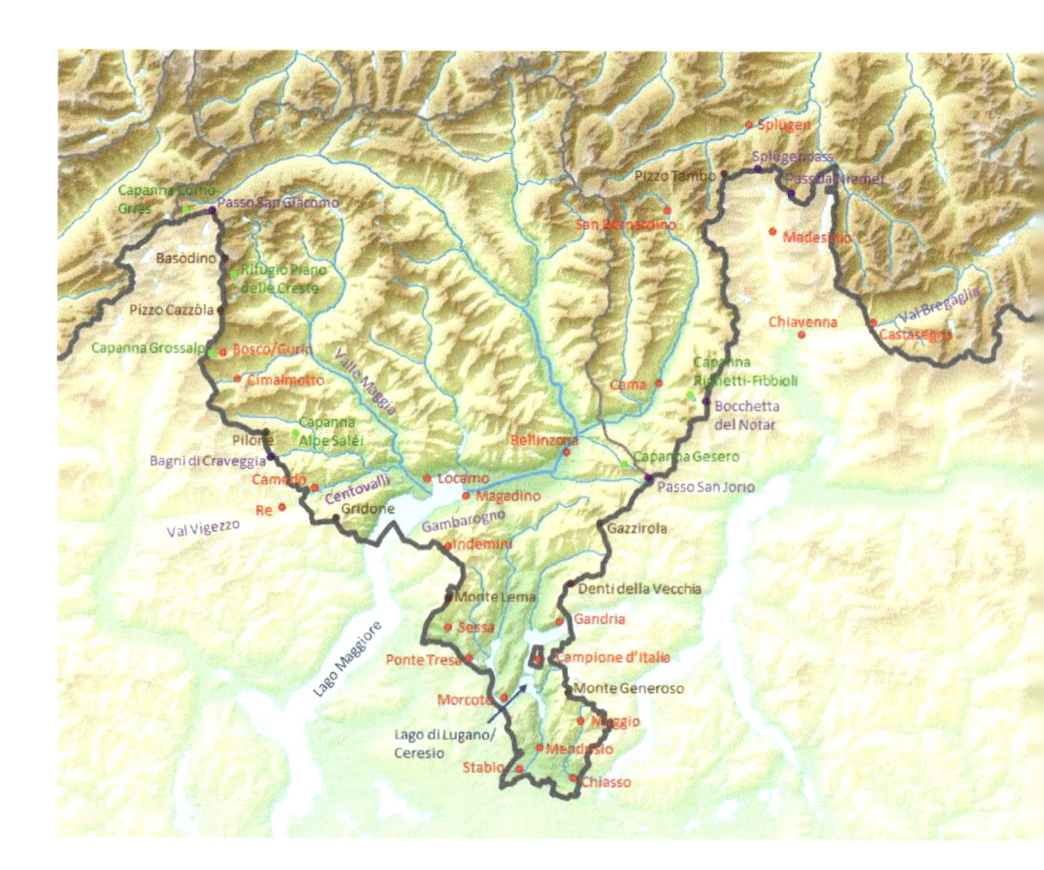

Nona had spent the night with us at the Corno-Gries Hut. I had asked her to pick up the car on the road below and meet us the next evening in Bosco / Gurin. She had to do almost 100 km in all. The last part, the climb to Bosco / Gurin from the Valle Maggia, gave her a first experience of narrow mountain roads, with hairpin bends and going past postal buses! She managed very well!

The next day was again sunny and beautiful. Off at around 7 a.m., we had to leave the red / white path to follow another one marked blue / white, which means a more alpine trail, often without a proper path, over scree and boulder fields. We crossed two cols and a summit in this way, and in the end the boulders finally got the better of me! I didn't really know how, but I twisted my left knee. As a result, I had to slow down and the last hour to the Grossalp Hut was quite painful. Nona welcomed us at the hut. She had driven my car (with the two-seater kayak on the roof) to Bosco / Gurin as planned and then she climbed the 700 m vertical height to the hut with food for us. There were people on the hut terrace (there is a chairlift!), enjoying the sun. Little by little, everyone went down to the village and we were almost alone for dinner and overnight.

Below Pizzo Cazzòla

Boulder field with no path

Some history

Bosco / Gurin was colonised in 1240 by Walser from the Upper Valais. It is mentioned for the first time in 1253 when the church was consecrated. Very isolated until the twentieth century, the inhabitants kept their dialect and the Alemannic culture, for example the names of localities and the distinctive style of houses. They had their contacts more with Val Formazza in Italy and the Upper Valais. It is the only German-speaking municipality in the canton of Ticino, although the use of German has fallen sharply in the last 50 years (82% of the inhabitants were German speakers in 1970, compared to only 33% in 2000, according to federal statistics). The municipality was attached to the canton of Lugano between 1798 and 1803, and to the canton of Ticino since 1803. The double name expresses the Italian and German languages, and the names of the pass connecting the Valle di Bosco / Gurin to Val Formazza show this very well: Passo di Bosco and Guriner Furggu.

We must continue, despite the sprained knee

My knee still did not allow me to go down the 400 m vertical height to the village, so I went to the upper station to take the chairlift (Peter and Nona came down on foot). There is no pharmacy in the village, only a tiny store where I got a bandage. On the other hand, a hotel gave me a package of anti-inflammatory pills, found almost by luck in their first aid kit.

I could then envisage a small stage on foot, with the knee bandaged, and using a ski pole lent by Nona (I had not used any so far). So Peter and I went up on the chairlift to pick up our gear from the hut. From there we reached Cimalmotto, a hike of about ten kilometres done in 3 hours. The weather was dull and rainy with a lot of wind, and all the summits were in the clouds. My knee held up pretty well, which gave me more confidence for the future.

In Cimalmotto I had booked accommodation in an agritourism site. It was a nice find – a farm-cum-dairy that offers a dormitory, small apartments or huts and a small campsite. They also run a small shop selling farm produce and other local products, all "organic". The place is beautiful. We were happy to stay in the dormitory, set in the attic of a barn, which we had for ourselves. Nona came by car from Bosco / Gurin, a trip of about fifteen kilometres of winding, narrow roads.

We plan the next meeting place

The next day I started walking again, with two ski sticks and an elastic bandage around the knee. I was a little slow going downhill on some stony trails, but otherwise I walked without any problem. A friend had warned me that it is almost impossible to make progress off the marked trails in Ticino below 2000 m without losing a lot of time and energy because of the vegetation – mainly small juniper trees, blueberry bushes and rhododendrons – and we had just experienced it ourselves, when we strayed a bit and tried to get back onto the right path by cutting through the undergrowth. Subsequently we chose marked trails as close to the border as possible.

Further on we met a young man at an alp sawing tree trunks. He said they had been brought in by helicopter when we greeted him and congratulated him on his work. He spoke good English. There followed a long stretch of path on large stones laid in slabs, very pleasant for walking.

A rare pleasant path!

We passed a small mountain hut – without a warden but where it was possible to take drinks and put money in a box, which I used for a beer – and later arrived at a small col at the end of a short quite tough climb. It was with some emotion that we saw Lago Maggiore for the first time, still far away but identified without any doubt. It was very encouraging because we felt that we were moving forward. From this col we also climbed the Pilone before descending to the Alpe Saléi Hut, where we found Nona. She had taken the car in a side valley of the Centovalli and then climbed the 700 m vertical height to the hut to meet us; she also brought some ointment for massaging my knee!

Deep valleys

The goal of the next day, July 31st, was to reach the Centovalli, crossing the very deep Onsernone valley and an intermediate ridge. This hike required more than 2000 m descent, not the best thing for my knees, but they survived! Fortunately, we had lighter backpacks, no longer needing to carry rope, ice axe or crampons.

A consequence of these deep valleys is that this part of the frontier with Italy does not follow the watershed, but is often lower down on the Swiss side. The border was determined according to old agreements on grazing rights for sheep and cattle and access to these areas was easier from the Italian side over the passes than from the Ticino side up the deep valleys.

Today, however, access to the border in the Onsernone valley is easier from Switzerland because a road has been built. Here, right at the frontier in Italian territory, one can find the ruins of the Craveggia baths. The access road leads into Switzerland and only a few steep paths lead across to the Italian village of Craveggia in the main valley. A spring of hot water at 28°C was exploited in the Middle Ages and a building was erected in the early nineteenth century to accommodate bathers. Avalanches and successive floods later forced the site to be abandoned but one can still bathe in the only still existing basin.

The ruins of the Craveggia baths

Nona was waiting for us at Camedo village. She had found no suitable accommodation in this part of the Centovalli; the inns were either full or very expensive. So we looked in the Italian Vigezzo valley and found a nice hotel – Albergo Bellavista in Folsogno (municipality of Re) – which was quieter and cheaper.

It was raining on August 1st, the Swiss National Day. Bad luck for the traditional fireworks at night! We went to Locarno to wander around, see the town, drink coffee, buy maps at a kiosk, eat kebabs in the street, and so on. August 2nd was a beautiful day: it was the day to traverse the Rocce del Gridone and the Gridone itself. Peter and I climbed up opposite Camedo and were soon at the start of the imposing north face of the Rocce. A hunter, accompanied by two dogs, told us that the route was well signposted, not too difficult, with two fixed ropes at tricky places. In fact, we managed the face on small paths, ledges and some easily climbed slabs. There were three places with chains. We did it all quite fast, without roping up. We emerged onto the ridge and traversed the Rocce, an exciting route, often exposed but still well marked. The weather was fine, we were alone and were very happy.

Gridone summit: view of Lago Maggiore and Locarno

We were on the summit of Gridone, 2188 m, early in the afternoon. We found a lot of hikers there, maybe thirty people. It was Sunday! The descent to Lago Maggiore was almost exactly 2000 metres vertical distance on fairly steep trails, later on a road, which was quite frustrating because it did not go down very steeply and had a lot of hairpin bends; one covers many kilometres without losing much height.

We now had to cross Lago Maggiore. August 3rd was a beautiful day, calm and windless on the lake. Launching the 2-seater kayak was awkward; we needed to take it down a metal staircase leading from the main road behind the Italian customs post to a "beach" of rocks. Once in the water everything was fine and I noticed with pleasure that Peter had already kayaked. We arrived on a beautiful beach next to the frontier on the eastern shore, where Nona joined us a few minutes later. She took the opportunity to swim in the lake with Peter, while I sipped a beer . . .

Starting on Lago Maggiore

After loading the kayak onto the car, we began the ascent of the hills of Gambarogno. It was very hot; it was only when we left the forest some 1200 m higher that the air became cooler and more breathable. We crossed Monte Paglione and went down to a small col where we found Nona who had parked the car in Indemini village and climbed the approximately 360 m on foot. We continued all together for 15 minutes to Alpe Cedullo, a very nice agritourism site.

The next day was cloudy and foggy most of the day, so not too hot. We soon went through Indemini, which is at the end of the Italian Val Veddasca, 500 m north of the border. This village is interesting because it was very isolated for a long time. Until 1920 the only access to the village was on trails over the mountains of Gambarogno to the north or on a barely drivable track up the valley to the south. In 1920 a daring Swiss road was built over a col at 1395 m to ensure national access to the inhabitants of Indemini. On the other hand, the link with Val Veddasca in the south only dates from 1966. A postal bus connects the village to Magadino on Lago Maggiore by a winding road: no less than 132 turns and 38 hairpin bends!

But the isolation of Indemini may have helped preserve an authentic and homogeneous Ticino village whose houses are built with local gneiss, tiled with granite and adorned with beautiful wooden balconies.

Indemini

We climbed up opposite Indemini and continued on a good trail on the north-south ridge to Monte Lema. From here, we followed the frontier to the south to the village of Sessa. The last part of this descent, at the end of the day, was once again very tedious and frustrating because it was too flat – we only lost height very slowly, while covering kilometres of trail!

Car battery problem

The next day we hiked a couple of kilometres to the Tresa river that we followed along a pretty path to Ponte Tresa. Nona was waiting for us there, but there was a problem with the car – it did not start again after a stop of more than 15-20 minutes! It had already happened in Indemini but then she was able to leave because the car was parked on a slope. Now, nothing to be done, the battery was flat. We asked another tourist to help us, which he was happy to do, and the engine started with jump cables. We launched the kayak and started paddling on the Ceresio (the local name of Lake Lugano).

It took us an hour and a half to cover the 8.5 km to the customs post on the south shore, opposite Morcote. Towards the end we had a headwind and a lot of small waves coming from all directions, the result of heavy motorboat traffic. Most unpleasant!

Nona was already there but the car was not starting, once again! This time, an Italian border commuter helped us, saying that he had once had the same problem on a mountain pass in Switzerland and that people there had helped him as well. We drove straight to a small garage in Mendrisio. The mechanic checked, decided to change the battery but did not have the right model in stock. So he then sent us to another garage, much larger and better equipped, 1-2 km further on. We arrived there a little after 6 p.m. but they were still open and the first garage had already warned them of our arrival! Half an hour later we had a new battery and we were directed to a hotel opposite Mendrisio railway station.

A historical landmark

I was very sorry to have lost half a day. We decided to try to catch up. The problem with many hotels is that you cannot have breakfast very early, as opposed to mountain huts where it is often normal to breakfast at 4 or 5 in the morning. The Mendrisio hotel served breakfast from 7.00 a.m. so we started hiking only at 8.40. It was sunny and hot. The first climb in the forest was still pleasant. Then, heat wave conditions hit us. We passed a couple of villages and the hills behind Stabio. Here we came across an old frontier stone dated 1559, still in very good condition. It bore the inscriptions "Liga Helvetica" on one side and "Status Mediolani" on the other.

A little research on the internet later taught me that the southern part of Ticino, the Mendrisiotto, was annexed by the Switzerland of the XIII cantons in 1512 and the possession was confirmed by the Treaty of Fribourg (also called "treaty of perpetual peace") signed on November 29th, 1516, after the defeat of the Swiss at Marignano in September 1515 by the French King François 1st. After several wars between the kings of France and Spain, the Spanish domination of the Duchy of Milan (Mediolanum in Latin) was recognized in 1559 by the peace of Cateau-Cambrésis. So it was not until that year that frontier stones were placed around on the border of the Mendrisiotto.

A frontier stone dated 1559 – Swiss and Italian sides

The next highlight was the southernmost point of Switzerland, which is a few kilometres south of Chiasso. A wooden statue of Helvetia has been placed next to the frontier stone, in front of a 4-metre high fence that runs along the border, as well as a small platform with benches opposite. For which ceremony? We did not really appreciate these amenities and continued to Chiasso station where we met Nona. Nine hours of walking in all, for a distance of about 35 km: so we had caught up the half day lost yesterday.

The southernmost point of Switzerland, to the south of Chiasso

The case of the lost camera

Later in the evening Peter announced that he had lost his camera. He thought he had left it at the southernmost point of Switzerland that afternoon. There was no choice, we had to go back again before breakfast! So we left at 5 a.m. and I drove him to the closest village, from where Peter had to walk for about 15 minutes. He returned 45 minutes later, having found nothing and having lost his way in the forest on the way back. We were then back at the hotel in time for breakfast.

The next section goes from Chiasso up into the hills, first on small roads between villas and then on good trails. It was again very hot. We ran out of water and could not drink in fountains. Further on, we came to an isolated farm. There were people there and I asked for water for our flasks. They obliged readily and as they were having coffee after lunch, they invited us to join them. We talked with them for some time. In fact, it was a kind of summer camp – they had about ten teenagers from the canton for a week and would be leaving later in the afternoon. At the end of the day, Nona was able to pick us up on the road above Muggio.

I received a message from Sally (at home in Grandvaux) that the police in Mendrisio had Peter's camera! I phoned them, and yes, someone had found it near the railway station, and we could pick it up at the Town Hall, but not before Monday morning. So it was Nona who would have to collect it. But how was it that the police contacted Sally? Peter thought he must have left the camera next to the car (or even on the roof of the car) when he had looked for something at night. The person who picked it up must have written down the car number plate and informed the police when he handed in the camera. Peter only had his address in the United States on the camera. A stroke of luck!

On Saturday, August 8th, I planned to arrive at the Ceresio lake from the south, opposite Gandria and cross the lake by kayak. There is no car access to the south shore here, so it was Peter who had to pick me up by kayak from the north shore. So I started alone for the ascent of Monte Generoso, 1000 m higher. Two hours later, I was at the summit, 1700 m, in splendid weather. The upper station of the funicular was a huge building site, and the cogwheel train was out of service for the whole summer of 2015. Further on I was on the Italian side on a spur that descended in the forest 400 metres from the frontier. I came across small pillboxes and trenches dug during the First World War, with many explanatory panels. But they did not explain why these fortifications had been built so far from Austria-Hungary and facing the Swiss frontier! Had they been afraid of an attack by the Swiss?

Huge building site on Monte Generoso (August 2015)

Monte Generoso summit, 1700 m

Later I arrived at the top of an old funicular leading down to the Ceresio lake. It was decommissioned in about 1975, but I was able to go down the steps next to it, being careful not to stumble over branches, stones and steel cables that lay around everywhere. It was still more convenient and faster than going down in the forest. Down by the lake, I was soon picked up by Peter and we crossed to the north shore. Peter and Nona had found a small hotel nearby in Italy, where we spent a nice evening.

Old funicular at Lanzo d'Intelvi

Circuit of the enclave of Campione d'Italia not possible

On the Sunday I had planned to go round the Italian enclave of Campione, 2-3 km on the lake by kayak and 3-4 km on land. We arrived at the border where I had hoped to be able to launch the kayak at a place marked "Lido" on the maps. But it was private property, a block of luxury apartments, and a caretaker who spoke only German forbade us formally to cross the 50 metres of land, even after knowing my project. She also said that the whole shoreline was private property and that it would be necessary to return to a public beach further away (which would have given almost 2 km more to paddle). She also informed me that the land border behind and above the villas and apartments was strangled by vegetation and almost inaccessible in many places: in fact, behind us, opposite the lake, there was a continuous row of houses and there was no trace of any path near the border, just a few alleys that went up the steep slope in hairpin bends. At the other end of Campione, in the Swiss village of Caprino, it was the same story. It was depressing and I decided to leave out Campione completely – we would have lost too much time to go round it, with a lot of detours.

In the afternoon Peter and I climbed from Gandria to the village of Brè, where Nona picked us up by car. This would save us 500 m of vertical height the next day. The weather was gloomy all day and the weather forecast was not bright for the next few days.

A very long day – arrival at the hut at night

The Monday turned out to be a very long day – 12 hours of hiking not including the stops, and reaching the mountain hut after dark. Why? We had to arrive at the Gesero Hut at the extremity of the Ticino, above Bellinzona. It is accessible by car (toll road) and I asked Nona to take it after going to Mendrisio in the morning to fetch Peter's camera. Also, it would be the last night with us for her.

From Brè we followed pleasant paths in the forest, mainly uphill, then passing the aptly named Denti della Vecchia (teeth of the old woman), a series of well-known limestone peaks, past two mountain huts, where we were above the tree line. Then came the gently sloping climb up Gazzirola, 2116 m, then a tedious ridge to a small col. We had covered about 30 km and it was already 5:30 p.m. There was no time to lose!

I may have made a mistake here by choosing a path on the Swiss side, which was a little longer and went down 100 metres more compared to a path on the Italian side (there was nothing on the jagged ridge itself), but we will never know if the latter way would have been faster. In any case, we had to climb almost 400 metres up to the Col San Jorio before a long almost horizontal traverse by which time it was already dark. For the last 30-40 minutes, we followed an unpaved road down to the hut – thankfully, it was easy to follow even in the dark. Peter did not want to use his headlamp to avoid being dazzled, and I did not have a torch with me that day! Nona was at the hut (with Peter's camera) and the friendly hut warden gave us a good meal, even as late as 9.30 p.m.

The next morning I drove down into the valley to find additional supplies and maps – without much success for the maps because the nearest bookstore was closed due to holidays. That afternoon Nona went down to Bellinzona, where she left the car and took the train to Milan, ready for the flight to Vancouver the next day. Peter and I only started hiking in the afternoon, carrying sleeping bags in order to bivouac en route. We climbed up close to the tripoint Ticino-Grisons-Italy and then followed the ridge and partly the Alta Via del Lario to the north, in sunny and warm weather, which we greatly appreciated. Around 8 p.m. we bivouacked on a grassy ledge at 2200 m under a small cliff on the Italian side. Peter and I slept quite well, despite the stones and clumps of grass, and even though the sleeping bags tended to slide down. We did not have a stove – this was planned – and there was only water and biscuits for breakfast, which is why we left very early! Indeed, we were already on our way at 6:20 a.m.

The day's trails were well signposted, but sometimes difficult to find, especially in the stony areas where there was no visible track and when the paint marks were some distance away and often hidden in the shade of large stones and boulders. A small col on a ridge had chains on both sides, which gave some interest. Later, we arrived at Capanna Como, with no warden and occupied by a group of young people, who kindly gave us a beer.

An awful trail

Almost two hours later we were at a small col called Bocchetta del Notar. The descent from this col was the worst "trail" I have ever experienced. It was well marked with red / white paint, but this only gave the general direction. The "path" was often non-existent, or descended in steep grass, blueberry and rhododendron bushes, or through shrubs or scree. But the worst was the long grass that covered a narrow track where people had walked. This long grass hid all other obstacles such as holes, stones (often covered with moss), shrub roots or steep slippery ground, with some brambles and ferns to complete the picture. Impossible to go fast, each step had to be taken carefully so as not to stumble or fall. Further down, the marks led to steeper rocks or grass, where there were rusty chains to help, often hidden under the long grass.

Peter in action   The mother of all bad paths!

Eventually the slopes became less steep and we ended up next to the Lagh de Cama (where Peter swam). A few minutes later we arrived at the nice Capanna Righetti-Fibbioli (Alp del Lago). There was no mobile phone network at the last col or the hut, but I was allowed to call home with their phones connected to a special aerial.

The next day was August 13th, my birthday! Sally had arranged to meet me in Splügen where she wanted to come with our son Roger. She could drive again and had booked rooms for the night at the village of Splügen for both of us as well as for Peter and Roger. An appointment not to be missed! We had agreed to meet at the Splügen Pass in the late afternoon.

It was a matter of getting away from the hut early to go down to the village of Cama, having a coffee and then the postal bus to Bellinzona. Nona had sent us an SMS explaining where she left the car and we duly found it.

We drove through the San Bernardino road tunnel to Splügen and the Splügen Pass. From this pass, we began the climb to Pizzo Tambo around midday. Without a heavy backpack I gained height quite rapidly. Halfway up I waited for Peter but he didn't appear (in fact, he had turned back, perhaps suffering from altitude). I continued alone to the summit, on a good trail. When I came down again to the pass a little before 5 p.m., I found a reception committee! My dear wife Sally, Roger and Peter, were there and welcomed me with a bottle of Prosecco and a birthday cake. A great surprise! Roger had also brought me a present – a large relief map of Switzerland, very relevant and well chosen! Later, we all dined together at the Hotel Suretta in Splügen.

Prosecco and birthday cake!

The Splügen Pass (2113 m) marks the Italian-Swiss border since the return in 1797 of the Valtellina to the Cisalpine Republic by Napoleon. Before the construction of the large Alpine tunnels, this pass was a busy passage with a large volume of goods (2000 mules per month). This intense activity gave rise to a prosperous economy. For those travellers in transit who had crossed the pass unhindered, the further descent to Thusis via the Via Mala represented a new ordeal . . .

Unlike some other Alpine passes, such as the Simplon, where road improvements have made their crossing easy, the 65 km long Splügen Pass road is a challenge. If you drive from Chiavenna to Splügen in bad weather, you will remember it for a long time. Sally (and Roger) did just this!

The formidable Splügen pass road

We emerge from the fog in the wrong valley!

The next day was one of which I am not proud. At the end we finished in the wrong valley! How? Bad route finding? For the blog of the day, August 14th, I chose as title "Incomplete Maps". But let's start at the beginning.

There was a storm the previous night and it rained sporadically all day. Sally and Roger offered to take my car (still with the kayak) to the Bregaglia Valley where we should be in two days. After a lot of sorting clothes, maps, food, etc. we all left for the Splügen Pass. Sally and Roger left us here and each drove a car to the Swiss customs post at Castasegna where they dropped off my car, before heading home. Sally later complained that the descent to Chiavenna was appalling – rain, poor visibility, hairpin bends and lots of traffic.

At the Splügen Pass there was a very strong cold wind and a little rain. No summit was possible, so we took a path across to Rifugio Bertacchi. Here we waited for the end of a storm and torrential rain, and left again a little after 2 p.m.

Two very recent Swiss maps (2009 and 2014) showed a marked path from the Passo di Niemet, half an hour from the hut, to a second pass into the next valley, *without any other paths*. At the top of the climb, we were in the clouds and exposed to very strong wind and driving rain, and we followed the red / white and yellow marks. Under these conditions, we missed a turn-off. I should have been more critical, because we had met two other hikers half an hour before the top. They explained to us that there was a first pass, followed by a descent and a second pass for which it was necessary to go up again 30-40 metres. Later, I wondered where this second pass was and should have looked at the GPS. But the hikers had given no indication of the distances, there was still wind, rain and fog and we were religiously following the markers, so what's the point?

It was only later, much lower, when we came out of the clouds – very wet – that we gradually realised that something was wrong – too late! No option but to go on to the village of Madesimo (as it was called) and find a place to sleep. We settled in an albergo where I found a tourist brochure with marked hiking trails. It showed the two trails that separated shortly after yesterday's first pass. I would never have thought that a tourist brochure with red lines on a relief map could be more accurate than the official Swiss map!

August 15th was again a rainy day. I had forgotten that this day was "ferragosto", a holiday in Italy, although this did not change anything for us. The hotel in Madesimo was fine and our stay allowed us to dry out all our clothes and gear. We took the bus to Chiavenna where we had time to do some errands and eat ice cream. A second bus (Swiss postal bus) took us to Castasegna, the first Swiss village. We immediately found my car and a small hotel where we settled in. We spent most of the afternoon watching the rain, planning the next few days and updating our blogs. Dinner in a pizzeria just across the border in Italy, 2 minutes from the hotel.

Castasegna marked the end of a stage. The next few days would be more dramatic and unpredictable, bringing changes to our plans.

The case of the missing car keys

Sally and Roger had left my car in a small car park near the Swiss customs post before returning home. I had asked them to hide the keys in a special place under the car. A day later I opened the car with the spare keys, having forgotten my instructions! Two to three weeks later I asked them where the keys were and we realised that they had been left in the parking lot in Castasegna. Too bad!

Another month later, while visiting my garage near home, the manager said to me "Ah, we got your keys" and gave me an envelope, which had been hanging in his office for at least five weeks! I could not believe it! They had been posted in Castasegna by an Italian, perhaps a frontier commuter. This good Samaritan had written his address on the small parcel, without making any other comment. So I wrote him a short thank you letter, enclosing 50 euro note.

Smuggling

It is likely that the well-known case of the exfiltration of silkworms and their eggs from China to the Byzantine Empire by two Nestorian monks around the year 550 AD is one of the first examples of international smuggling (even if there are other theories).

Every time there is a border, official or not, separating two regions that are different politically or economically, there will be differences in price or availability of goods. These differences can result from differences in taxation (taxes, customs duties, VAT) or in subsidies, or in agricultural or industrial conditions, or in wages. Whatever the reason, these differences will lead individuals and businesses to source from where the conditions are most favourable. Entrepreneurs will try to make a profit by buying goods cheaply on one side of a border and selling more expensively on the other side. The nature of the "goods" has changed over time, depending on conditions that have changed as well. Contraband is essentially a phenomenon of inequality. The word contraband comes from "contra bannum", that is, against the law.

This phenomenon was already present in past centuries, despite heavy penalties for those who were caught: branding with hot irons, years in galleys, or worse, in France. But nothing could stop the smugglers from crossing the borders by winding and steep paths, in one direction or the other.

The Swiss border has also known – and still knows! – traditional smuggling, which involves taking goods across the border without paying customs duties, usually by land or by water. For centuries, salt, sugar, meat, alcohol, matches, watch components as well as fabrics crossed the Swiss border, sometimes legally, sometimes less so.

During the First World War, difficulties in obtaining food in Switzerland led to a flow of contraband from Italy to Switzerland. The smugglers were trying to trade first necessity goods such as sugar, coffee, rice and salt.

During the Second World War, people were mainly involved in the trafficking of food. In addition, local women also risked their lives by guiding French resistance fighters and Jewish refugees on the old smuggling routes. In the post-war years, goods such as rice and coffee moved from Italy to Switzerland, while alcohol and cigarettes moved in the opposite direction.

Today, it is mainly meat, deli meats and dairy products that enter Switzerland illegally because they are significantly cheaper on the other side of the border, while cigarettes and electronics are exported illegally. Different VAT rates are often a reason for smuggling!

We must also mention the illegal export of weapons from Switzerland, as well as the trafficking of drugs and human beings (illegal immigrants).

All around the Swiss border, there are notice boards, names of places such as cols or inns, anecdotes, legends or historical facts that bear witness to this activity. These accounts often have heroic, even romantic aspects. Almost everywhere, hikes are proposed, guided or not, on the theme "smugglers' paths".

For example:

- Les Echelles de la Mort (The Ladders of Death), on the Doubs

There is also an explanatory panel covering the subject along the Doubs (see picture on page 14)

- Skilift Contrebandiers, below the Tour de Don (near Châtel in France)
- Passo del Contrabbandiere, in the Binntal
- A via ferrata (no longer maintained) that follows the old smugglers' path to Gondo
- Percorso dei Contrabbandieri, Maloja
- Schmugglerweg, Germany near Rheinau

But better known is probably the Customs Museum in "Cantine di Gandria". This neat-looking museum is a little gem that deserves a visit, which will allow one to learn more about the phenomenon of smuggling. Although small, the establishment has modern technology and captivating exhibitions. From Cantine di Gandria, the customs officers monitored the contraband traffic until 1921 (due to the isolated location, only unmarried customs officers were stationed there).

To get there, it is best to take the boat from Lugano (frequent shuttles in the summer). Very recommendable: disembark at Caprino and follow the trail along the lake to the museum (about 40 minutes). For the return, the boat crosses the lake to Gandria and continues to Lugano. But one can also choose to return to Lugano by walking the olive tree path that has interesting information panels along it.

Some references

General

https://en.wikipedia.org/wiki/Smuggling_of_silkworm_eggs_into_the_Byzantine_Empire

http://www.silk-road.com/artl/silkhistory.shtml

http://www.hec.unil.ch/jusunier (Jean-Claude Usinier; search for "La grande Triche", see chapter 4)

Article about Franche-Comté in Via, September 2016

Increase in contraband from Germany, Article in 24 Heures, 12.02.2015

http://www.notrehistoire.ch/medias/2148 Smuggler dogs

https://en.wikipedia.org/wiki/Smuggling

http://www.heimatschutz.ch/uploads/tx_userzeitschrift/28_02_2008_f3.pdf

For the Customs Museum

https://www.ezv.admin.ch/ezv/en/home/the-fca/customs-museum-in-cantine-di-gandria--lugano/das-museum.html

Paths and hikes

http://www.lescheminsdelacontrebande.com/

https://www.j3l.ch/fr/V1615/les-chemins-de-la-contrebande-l-orlogeur

http://www.123chablais.com/FR_itineraire--itineraires--sur-les-pas-des-contrebandiers-morzine-champery-francesuisse--itineraire--csuijvrqgrcwz.html

http://www.klettersteig.de/klettersteig/schmugglerweg_gondo/1050

http://www.news.ch/Tessiner+Schmugglerwege+erleben+Renaissance/127018/detail.htm

http://www.luganomontebre.ch/index/en/contrebande/ (contains the following picture)

The Grisons, second part

From the Val Bregaglia to Samnaun

The canton of the Grisons (Graubünden in German) is not only the largest canton in Switzerland, it is also the canton with the longest international border, 466 km with Italy, Austria and Liechtenstein, most of which is mountainous or Alpine. I have divided the rest of the story of my adventures in the Grisons into two parts, which correspond to the sections done in 2015 and 2016. Let me say at the outset that I had accumulated delays, for various reasons, and that I was not able to finish the circuit without stopping for the winter. But for the moment everything was still fine!

In the morning of August 16th it was not raining but remained cloudy. We left the Val Bregaglia, for the long climb, soon on stony paths and scree to the Bocchetta della Tegiola. We passed by a bivouac hut and climbed to the highest pass of the day, Passo Porcellizzo, 2961 m, in light rain and fog. We arrived very wet at the mountain hut (Rifugio Gianetti) a little after 6 p.m. The forecasts for the next day were quite good.

Unfortunately, these forecasts were not correct! When we left the hut at 7 a.m., the sky was completely overcast and it had rained during the night. We headed for the spur which is the "voie normale" up Pizzo Badile. Later it started to rain again gently and the fog covered the top of the mountain. Not keen on climbing wet and cold rocks, we turned back.

What was to be done with the rest of the day? Peter was happy to stay in the hut. As for me, I could not remain inactive. Seeing that the rain had stopped, I spent a few hours descending the 1,500 metres to the village of San Martino, where I wanted to find an ATM to fill my wallet with Euros. The hut warden's wife assured me that there was one, in working order. In fact, it was wasted time. The ATM was out of order, a thunderstorm 3 days previously had damaged the connections, and the bank itself was closed.

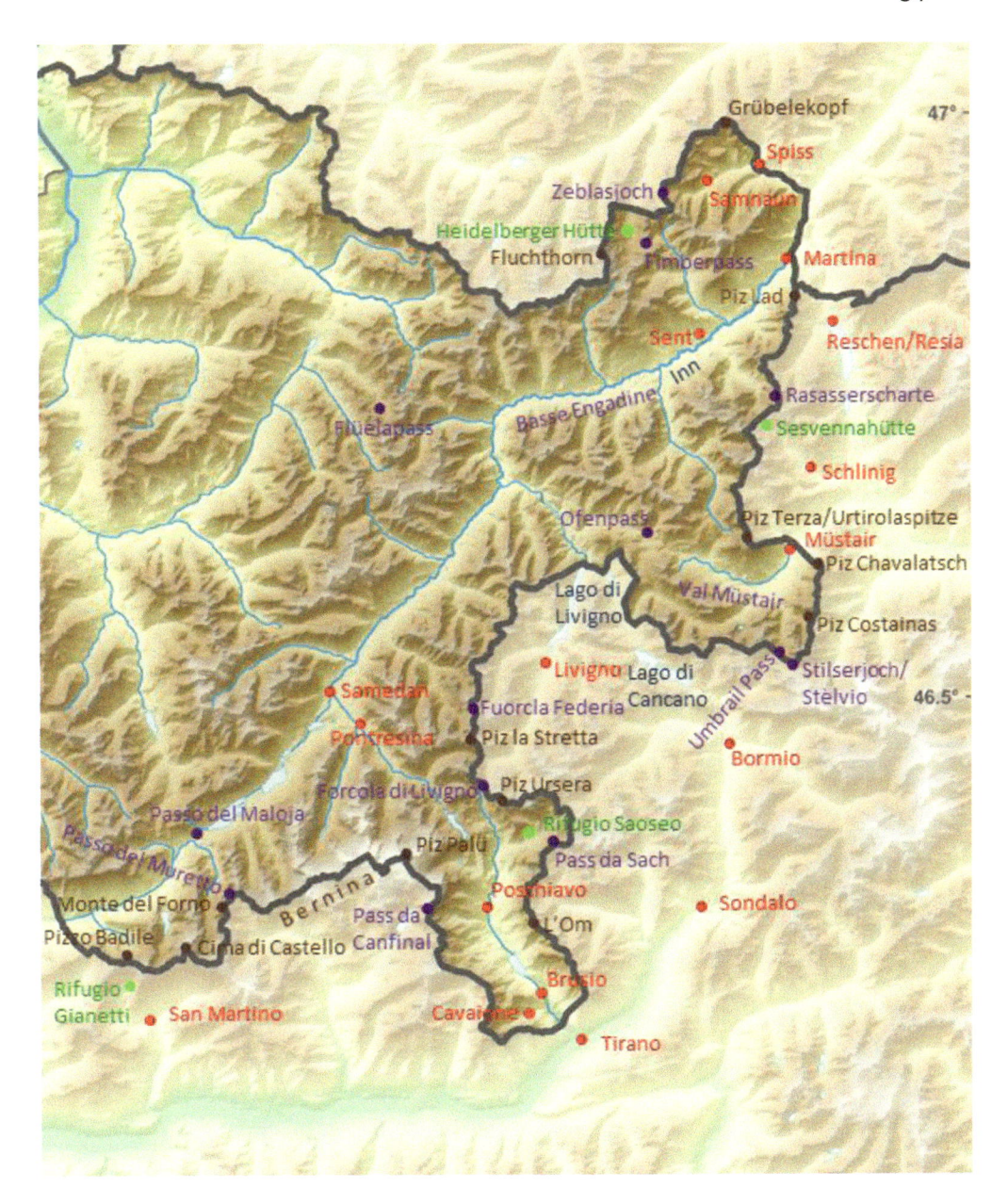

A most unfortunate incident

We did not know it yet, but August 18th was going to end dramatically and could easily have meant the end of my adventure. There were low clouds and some rain in the morning and we gave up all hope of doing the Pizzo Badile and other peaks.

Since Peter had to go down and leave the mountains the next day, to be able to reach Milan two days later and return to the United States, we decided to hike a leg of the "GR" Via Roma trail to the next mountain hut. Fate decided otherwise.

An hour and a half after our departure from the hut, we were in a rather steep boulder field on a path that zigzags up to a col. I tried to take a shortcut over a slab, but my foot slipped and I fell very awkwardly, slamming my face against a boulder. It was a hard jolt, I saw blood on the stones, got up and noticed that my face was hurting me on the left side. In fact, there was an injury right next to my left eye and a lot of blood. My right thumb was also all bloody. My first reaction was anger – how could I have been so stupid and awkward at the same time? And I let slip some nasty words!

Peter was 2-3 minutes behind me – he had stopped to take pictures – and a German couple who was in front came to help me. They kindly put a bandage on my cheek and head and urged me to return to the hut. The man even took a picture of my face on his mobile phone to show me the damage. My eye was starting to swell (black eye!). So I had to resign myself to return to the hut.

Back there, I explained what had happened and asked them to clean my face a bit, which they did, telling me that it did not look too serious; they were really very kind. I thought of going down to the valley again, but suddenly the hut warden came: "The helicopter will be here in ten minutes!" Impossible to refuse and I knew in my heart that this was the only solution. Peter decided to redo the route we did two days ago backwards to find the car. I said it would be long, leaving only at noon, but he insisted. So I took the rope into my rucksack to lighten his.

And already the helicopter was visible, approached quickly and landed. Everything was moving very fast. Goodbye in a hurry, good luck, etc.

In the helicopter they put me on a stretcher, a man took my rucksack (he was not doing anything else), a nurse on the right was interviewing me – what exactly happened, where, did I lose consciousness, were there other people involved, etc? Not easy to understand with the sound of the engines and then answer in Italian! At the same time another nurse (on the left, where I could hardly see anything) took a blood sample, measured my pulse and blood pressure and also – I discovered later – did an electrocardiogram. The journey took 20-30 minutes, to go to a hospital in Sondalo, between Tirano and Bormio.

There, I was made to wait a good while on a stretcher with an uncomfortable collar around the neck (in case there was a spinal injury) and I had to fill out forms. In due course, I was brought into the radiology department for scans and x-rays. Then another long wait, during which I had time to think and meditate. I blamed myself – why did I decide to take this shortcut, which was not necessary at all? And the future? According to the severity of my injuries, did this accident mean the end of my journey, or only longer or shorter delays? I started to wonder if I could even finish my circuit this year, or not at all. I also had time to call my son Roger to explain what had happened, but I did not want him to tell Sally at this stage; she was at the time on vacation in Spain with grandchildren.

Finally, the doctor came and told me about the results of the tests: the brain, the left eye, the neck, the spine, and so on were all in order, but the three bones that surround the eye orbit were fractured but not displaced, which might require further treatment. You can imagine how relieved I was! I chose to follow up near my home in Switzerland and I had to sign a discharge form. They treated the wound – a few stitches – gave me a detailed medical report and pictures of x-rays on a CD and let me go.

Back home, hospital in Lausanne

Roger had already contacted an old friend and ski touring colleague, Fritz Hagmann, who lives in Pontresina. He immediately offered to pick me up at the hospital. He was aware of my project, but I had a pang of bad conscience because I had not informed him at the beginning, thinking to wait until I was closer to the Grisons. Afterwards, I forgot, but fortunately a mutual friend had already informed him.

Fritz very kindly fetched me at Sondalo at 6 p.m.; it was a 90-minute drive in each direction. He did not reproach me in any way but simply said that he had also had mountain incidents in his youth. When I thanked him, he answered disarmingly, "You would have done the same for me." In my emotional state, probably still suffering from shock and greatly relieved to have been released from the hospital, his reply brought tears to my eyes. His statement was absolutely true, but I could not imagine ever having the opportunity to help him out in the same way. In the end I spent the night in his flat with him and his wife Ursulina.

Meanwhile, Peter had made his way back to the Val Bregaglia, but he was very tired, took two falls in the dark – fortunately not too serious – and reached the car at 1 a.m.! He slept a little in the car. In the meantime there had been phone calls between Roger, Peter and Fritz to agree on meeting places and times. Peter drove to Fritz's residence in Pontresina, arriving around 11 a.m. Roger took a day off work, left at 5.30 a.m. and arrived in Pontresina just after Peter.

After a nice lunch together with Fritz and Ursulina, Roger brought Peter and me home – over 11 hours' drive in total, a great performance, not to mention the day off work. My car, with the two-seater kayak on the roof, stayed in Pontresina. Peter was going to take the train to Milan the next day to be ready to return to the United States the day after. I regretted his departure, despite my accident. He had been a wonderful companion. He would have liked to have climbed more summits, but returned happy.

I got an appointment very quickly at the main hospital in Lausanne. A lady doctor from the Department of Maxillofacial Surgery, after reading the report made in Sondalo and doing some tests, confirmed that I had no functional disorder and that there was no need to operate. The fractures were "normal" for this type of accident and the bones were well aligned. But she wanted to see me in a week when all the swelling was gone. My GP should remove the stitches in a few days. So I decided that it was not worth going back to the Grisons for another 2-3 days. Better to rest a little and eat well – in fact, I had lost about 6 kg since the beginning of June! Too bad for the week lost but I should be happy to have had a lot of luck and because the damage was in the end not too bad. The accident could have led to much more serious consequences!

<u>A new start</u>

To start again in the mountains of the Bregaglia and Bernina massifs I needed a mountain guide. I tried to get one in Pontresina for the next Saturday or Sunday, but they were all already taken – a weekend with good weather. But I could have somebody for Monday, August 31st, for at least two days. So I left for Pontresina on Saturday, August 29th, with a lot of luggage, to enjoy the hospitality of Fritz and Ursulina once again.

So what should I do on the Sunday? I decided to use this day to cover a section of easier frontier, without too heavy a backpack, and opted for the 2100 metre climb from the Val Poschiavo to the first summit of the chain to the east. Here the border goes straight up from the frontier post. It crosses several cliffs which could be avoided on paths just inside Switzerland. It was hot and it took me more than 5 hours to reach the highest point; the whole upper section was without a path, on steep grass and on scree. The view overlooking Tirano is superb. Then, I started the frontier ridge to the north but I had to turn back after about 2 kilometres because of large blocks and vertical slabs that were impassable for me without a rope.

View of Tirano

I descended to a village called Viano, which is perched on the side of the valley. I went into a small restaurant to ask for the postal bus timetable. But there is no timetable! Instead, you phone and the little yellow bus arrives 20 minutes later. I was the only passenger. The journey of several kilometres, on a narrow road, partly cut into the cliff and with countless hairpin bends, led to Brusio station. The price of the special trip, with a half-fare card: CHF 2.20, that is the normal fare! Fritz told me later that this is standard practice here and cheaper for the postal bus company than offering an official timetable. I took the 5-minute train ride from Brusio to collect the car and return to Pontresina.

The guide's office here had suggested I traverse the Cima di Castello, accessible from its northern side, and arranged a guide, Lukas. We met at 6.30 a.m. in the large car park just below the Maloja pass. Lukas left his car there and we went to the Albigna cable car, where we took the first gondola (only 8 places) at 7.00 a.m. We first climbed to the Capanna da l'Albigna from the upper cable car station. This mountain hut had special significance for me, because I had camped just below it with my brother Rolf in 1962!

The rest of the climb was uneventful, but the way to the summit took us over a crevassed glacier and Lukas had asked the hut warden to show him the best route on a map. This worked well and we found the best way through without once having to retrace our steps. After the summit, the route to the Forno Hut went down another very crevassed glacier and again Lukas found the best (the only?) safe way in an almost supernatural way, aided by the sketch of the hut warden. But he had also examined the glacier from the summit and had taken a picture that he later used to find the way.

Cima di Castello summit   Forno glacier

Down on the main glacier, we had to walk some 4 km on hard ice. Although the glacier was fairly flat, the surface was so irregular and furrowed with meltwater streams that our progress was rather slow. The hut is located about 250 metres above the level of the glacier, which was tiring at the end of the day, but offered superb views. It had been a long day, with more than 10 hours on the move.

The weather forecast was not good for the next afternoon, so we chose to take in the Monte del Forno, an easy mountain with a marked trail leading to the summit, albeit with a few chains, and requiring neither ice axe nor crampons. We started in cloudy and windy conditions, trying not to waste too much time. We arrived at the summit quite easily, went down by the Passo del Muretto on the border, and arrived at the car park at Maloja at 3 p.m. just as the rain started!

The next day it rained all morning and a good part of the afternoon in Pontresina, with all the mountains hidden in the clouds. I went to the Guides' office to discuss the future. They explained to me that the problem was fresh snow on open crevasses so that many trails through the glaciers were now too dangerous. Nevertheless, I tentatively booked a guide for the following Monday, 5 days away, to cross at least Piz Palü and Bellavista; all the forecasts agreeing on good weather for that day.

Around Val Poschiavo

In the meantime, I decided to spend another 2-3 days on the border around Poschiavo. My problem was being alone and having the car (with the kayak still on the roof!). I had to make small "loops", getting as high as possible by car and coming back to the same place to get it back. All of this involved substantial drops, with less time for the border itself, especially because the days were now getting shorter and shorter.

One day I left the car at Brusio station and took a path (unmarked but shown on the maps) that leads up to the village of Cavaione. It was covered with vegetation in places and I lost time by making my way through brambles. But the old path was there and could be followed quite easily. In the village, after about 90 minutes, I asked a lady aged 73 whether they had a bar there. No, there was no longer any bar or café, but she would happily make me a coffee! I gladly accepted and we chatted for a few minutes. I mentioned the "sentiero brutto" that I had just taken and she reproached me because it was dangerous and should not be used anymore. She told the usual story of young people who no longer want to work in the fields or even live in mountain villages. They move to larger centres, leaving only the older people in the villages.

By mid-afternoon I had reached a col on the border; from where a path and a very nice mountain bike track led down just on the Italian side of the frontier. Later, on a steep forest trail on the Swiss side, there were many mushrooms everywhere; the recent rainy days had certainly allowed them to develop under excellent conditions.

Shepherds' hut		Parasol mushroom, *Macrolepiota procera*

Chamois hunters

Another day I drove up to an alp called Motta, 1700 m, above Poschiavo town, to make a circuit on the border that included the crossing of the Om, 2789 m (the name is derived from the Italian "uomo"). It was sunny all day.

I experienced an interesting incident: after about an hour and a half I met two hunters, each of them pulling down the corpse of a chamois behind him, on its back and headfirst, in the long grass which covered the path at this point. Presumably they would carry their prey on their shoulders when the path was stony. They greeted me "Bon di" but apart from that they paid no attention to me, and I did not dare to take a picture. Was it the hunting season? Were they poachers? At an alp lower down there had been two men drinking wine (at midday) and I now wondered if they had been waiting for the hunters.

Later, Fritz Hagmann informed me: it was indeed the hunting season and the hunters had to kill a female chamois first before looking for other game.

It had been raining hard for most of the night and in the morning the main peaks were either hidden in the clouds or covered with fresh snow down to about 2400 metres. I chose the Pass da Canfinal because there was a marked trail and because you can drive up to 2080 metres! This was already quite an adventure, on small unpaved forest roads, and many farmers or local shepherds would have wondered where I would find white water for kayaking! The weather was good and there was even a bit of sun – until it started raining and snowing again around 3 p.m., but by that time I was down again. There was a fair amount of snow on the pass (2628 m), hiding all paths and markings, so I could not attempt any summits.

Pass da Canfinal

Once again I met two hunters – I was already going down and they were watching me from behind a large boulder. Shortly after, a shot rang out and echoed around the valley. Hunters must be within 100 metres of their target, so I must have gone very close to a chamois without seeing anything. And the hunters would have had to wait for me to pass. On the other hand, the whole area was teeming with marmots – I heard many of their warning squeals and I even glimpsed one or two rushing into their holes.

I am ill!

After 4 nights in hotels in Pontresina and Poschiavo, I was welcomed again by Fritz and Ursulina. And the good news: it would be nice on Monday the 7th, so the climb and the crossing of the Piz Palü were confirmed!

On Sunday morning I was happy and looked forward to the climb ahead. I did not yet know that everything would be upset within 24 hours. I took the cable car to the Diavolezza in the afternoon and was waiting to meet the guide. At supper time, I had a little fever, felt tired and had no appetite. The Berghaus ("hotel") had no first aid kit and none of the other guides had aspirins. Breakfast was planned around 4 a.m. In fact I had a short episode of shivering the day before when with Fritz and Ursulina, which I attributed to the cold. I should have treated it as an alarm signal or warning.

At 4 a.m. I had to tell the guide that I had to give up – I had slept very badly and felt weak and lethargic, having trouble even climbing the stairs. I drank some tea and we arranged to meet at 7 o'clock for a second breakfast. Then we took the first gondola down at 8.30. It was a beautiful day. Such a pity! I went to the Guides' office and gave them a lot of money. I ended up at Ursulina's (Fritz was away) who immediately took me to a doctor. The lady diagnosed an infection of the kidneys and prescribed an antibiotic and rest. I slept all afternoon, swallowed some soup (still no appetite) and went to bed very early.

The next day I slept most of the day! I could even eat a little. But the following day, I still had some fever and did not feel well. The doctor then sent me to Samedan hospital for further investigation. There they quickly saw that my bladder was too full and was not emptying properly. They inserted a catheter to empty it, made me swallow more antibiotics and kept me for the night. Obviously this setback was a big disappointment for me and once again I did not know if I would be able to continue my circuit of the Swiss frontier. But at the same time I was happy to be in good hands and looked after by professionals.

To my great and pleasant surprise, Sally came into my room the next morning! She had arrived by train the day before, quite late, and was happy to find a room in front of Samedan station at 11 in the evening! I felt good, I had regained my appetite and I had no more fever. I had to stay one more night in the hospital before being allowed to go home. I was very grateful to Fritz and Ursulina for helping Sally and me over the last few days, and to all those who sent me messages of support following my blogs, all messages very much appreciated!

Back in Lausanne, the doctors confirmed that there was no problem with the kidneys but that I would have to undergo prostate surgery sooner or later. Subsequently, there were a lot of delays, sometimes frustrating, that allowed me to rest and eat a lot to regain some of the weight I had lost in previous weeks. In the end I had to wear a catheter (and have a bag of urine strapped to my left thigh) for more than three months, until the day of the operation in mid-December! This did not prevent me from continuing my tour as far as possible depending on the weather and snow conditions. There was no prohibition on walking – the doctors had even advised a little exercise! It was by now obvious that I was not going to finish the circuit this year but I was determined to do as much as possible before winter set in. Stopping was not an option for me, as long as I was physically able to continue!

Another start in October

So I returned to the mountains and Val Poschiavo only on October 1st. I climbed up to the Saoseo mountain hut, where I was lucky to get a room on my own, because of a large group of hikers from Ticino who had been placed in the dormitories.

The next day the weather was very cloudy. I left for the Pass da Sach. From around 2400 m, all the mountain slopes were covered with 5 – 15 cm of fresh snow, including the path (which was well marked and not too difficult to follow). But my progress was slower because of the slippery stones under the snow, which required more care. The cloud level remained around 2900 m all day and it rained a little in the afternoon. Under these conditions, no summit was possible. I could have been back at the hut for lunch, but I had the time and energy to traverse to a second pass on the frontier. In the evening, there was a very nice atmosphere in the hut – where the welcome was very warm and friendly – the Ticino group sang an impressive repertoire of songs in Italian, French and even Swiss German! The weather forecast for the next two days: rain!

Pass da Sach

Pass da Val Viola

In fact, the weather was not too bad. It had rained sporadically all night. I left the hut wearing all my rain gear, but it did not actually rain until around midday. No problem up to the first pass, but from there on the path (if there was one) was not marked and there was more and more snow, up to 30 cm at the top of Piz Ursera. Maybe I should not have tried, but the alternative would have been a huge detour. So my progress was slow, visibility was reduced to about 100 m in the fog, there was a cold wind and it was snowing. Winter conditions! Thanks to the GPS, I found my way to the top, wrote my name in the summit book and started the descent. Steep, with a lot of fresh, unconsolidated snow, into which I sank at every step. I knew that the way was feasible, having done it on skis from that side about fifteen years previously. Again, the GPS was essential and as I lost height there was less and less snow on the rocks and visibility improved. I finally came across a path with cairns and reached the frontier again just above the Forcola di Livigno. There, it was not snowing any more but it was raining sporadically.

Back at the car, I saw that the Bernina Pass road was closed due to a Porsche rally. So I used the time to have a coffee and take off all my wet clothes (and the boots – which had held up well, but were not able to cope with puddles and wet snow on the lower slopes). For me it was the end of the Val Poschiavo. I entered the Italian duty free zone of Livigno, where I found a cheap hostel.

It again rained a lot during the night and the weather was still sullen in the morning. After refuelling (0.92 cents/litre unleaded, duty free zone!), I drove to a small uninhabited shack at 2099 m on the road to the Forcola di Livigno. I was preparing for an outing when it started to rain very hard, so I listened to music in the car for an hour. Suddenly the rain stopped and the clouds seemed to be clearing somewhat. So go for it! I climbed quickly to La Stretta pass, with a light backpack. There was fresh snow from 2200 m, covering the path entirely from about 2300 m.

I had planned to continue up Piz la Stretta on a marked path, but everything was in the fog and I would have taken at least 3 hours there and back for the remaining 650 m, with fresh snow much deeper higher up. Besides, the sky was completely covered again (earlier on the climb, I had 2-3 minutes of sun and I saw my own shadow for the first time in 2 days!) The decision to turn back was quickly taken and the mountain congratulated me by sending me fresh gusts of wind and flurries of snow. I then headed for Pontresina to pay a quick visit to Fritz and Ursulina, then returned home in the afternoon.

Around Livigno

A week later I returned to Livigno to take my revenge on Piz la Stretta under good conditions. The snow line had risen to around 2800 m and the snow was hard, making walking easier.

After reaching the summit, I wanted to continue along the border to the north as far as possible. But the ridge did not look too safe under the snow; this ridge is not described in the guide (is it done?). I tried to go down the west ridge so I could reach the border further north. It is graded "peu difficile", but after going down a very steep snow slope I had to give up because of a band of vertical rocks, only 3-4 metres high, which seemed to have no weak points. So, back to the top, after wasting a good hour of my time. Then I found a cunning way around the ridge to the east, but needed to go down 400 m and up again, which cost me another 2 hours. The next stretch of the border to the north went quite fast; in fact, the hard snow cover made things easier.

I had to stop at Fuorcla Federia and go down the very long Federia valley to Livigno. The next summit would have been more difficult and I was running out of time. Sally and Roger had arrived in the afternoon and Roger was able drive up the valley to pick me up, which saved me walking the last 3 kilometres.

The next day – we are now October 12th – we went to Lago di Livigno near the Punt dal Gall dam, which is crossed by the border. I had carried out a reconnaissance two days before and even asked the lady at the toll booth for the Livigno tunnel (which connects Livigno with Switzerland, on the Ofenpass road) if I could put a kayak in the water near the entrance to the tunnel (without paying the toll) but it was a flat refusal, in an unpleasant way. She said that boats were prohibited near the dam for security reasons. So we launched the kayak and started paddling near the old Italian customs post a little further away from the dam. Roger and I paddled about 4 km across the lake. It was nice enough, with no wind, the water was unruffled, flat as a mirror, and the temperature pleasant. The landscape was also magnificent, the forest of already golden larches reaching right down to the lake. Forty minutes later Roger dropped me off near a path on the north shore just past the frontier. He went back alone in the kayak but had to paddle almost 6 km to find an easier place to get the boat out of the water. Later, he returned home to Grandvaux, while Sally took the road to Bormio, where she found accommodation for us both.

Lago di Livigno   Roger leaves me

I hiked about another 18 km on good roads or forest tracks on the Italian side of the border, to the Cancano dam, where Sally fetched me in the car. All this section could have been done by mountain bike. Indeed, I met two cyclists on this stretch, and only two hikers. It was no longer the tourist season!

The next day I started again just above the Cancano dam. It had rained a little during the night; in the morning the sky was completely covered, with shreds of clouds everywhere. The paths were quite pleasant and easy to follow (mountain bike trails everywhere), the visibility was very variable, with a lot of thick fog from 2400 m upwards (one could hardly see 50 metres). A few hours later Sally was waiting for me at the Umbrail Pass for a quick picnic and I hiked on up to the Stelvio Pass (or Stilfserjoch), at 2757 m the highest road pass in the Alps, and highlight of the Giro d'Italia cycle race. There was a lot of activity despite the fog: tourists and already skiers!

At the Umbrail Pass   Old Italian customs building

We settled into the friendly Hotel Genziana. Imagine our surprise when we woke up to find that it had snowed during the night: 10-12 cm at the Stelvio Pass (and on the car), and even more higher up, and the whole landscape plastered with fresh snow.

I had planned to do a high level trail from the Stelvio Pass to Piz Chavalatsch, then descend to Müstair. Despite forecasts that announced a quieter period, even slightly sunny until the end of the afternoon, the trek could not be attempted safely with 15-20 cm of fresh snow. The next two days would again bring bad weather. So, once again, we returned home, crossing the Umbrail Pass, the Ofenpass and Flüela Pass, hoping for a stable period of good weather later in the year.

From Stelvio to Val Müstair – and an incident that could have been very serious

We returned to the Stelvio Pass a week later. All the passes were open, and the roads dry, but the Stelvio was already closed on the Alto Adige side.

There was still some fresh snow on my planned path, so I agreed with Sally to call her after about an hour's hiking to let her know if I was going on or turning back. At the Stelvio Pass it was -6°C but the day looked good: no clouds, no wind. There was still 15-20 cm of fresh snow, less where it had blown off from the ridges and it had even disappeared in places. This was acceptable. So I called Sally to say that I would continue. A mistake! As I progressed northwards, the snow became deeper. For about a kilometre I could follow the tracks of an ibex herd but then it became harder and more tiring; I sank in up to my knees, sometimes to my hip between boulders. I crossed five summits in all. The climb up the last two proved easier; there was less snow between the rocks and I could follow the markings, visible in places. On the other hand, the technical difficulty was higher, "peu difficile" or even more, and in the descents, quite steep, I often sank in up to my thighs.

| Below Piz Cotschen | Piz Costainas – south face |

It was precisely while descending the northern ridge of Piz Costainas that I experienced an incident that could have been quite serious, perhaps making me spend the night in the mountains. On a steeper stretch, I decided to climb down backwards, that is facing the slope. I had an ice axe in one hand, a ski pole in the other. There must have been a little slab under the snow; suddenly I slid down about 2 metres, to sink in up to my thighs. But losing my balance I fell backwards! So I was stuck, head down, lying on my backpack, held by my legs that were stuck in the snow up to the knees. It was not unpleasant but I could not move! I did not have the strength to pull myself up. Only solution, remove the backpack. Having done this I could get up by pulling on the ice axe and the ski stick. I was about to succeed when the snow around my legs gave way and I slid another 2 metres on my back before I could turn round and stop at a place that was less steep. What do I see? My rucksack, which had been beside me, had taken advantage of its new-found independence and was rolling and sliding slowly in the snow down the slope on the Italian side, followed by my woolly hat, sliding on the surface of the snow. My first thought – "my mobile phone is in the rucksack!" I must get it back if I want to warn Sally. Down below, there was a steeper gully and even lower, quite far away, a snow-covered shelf. I told myself, okay, I'll go down to the col, from where I can traverse back and retrieve my rucksack.

But it stopped in the middle of the gully about 20 metres down, a strap must have got caught somewhere. The woolly hat had also stopped. So I went down the gully cautiously, trying not to send too much snow onto my bag, which could dislodge it and send it further down! I was soon there and could return with it. But the hat continued its slide and ended up too far down. In the end I lost only twenty minutes. And I put the mobile phone in an inside pocket of my jacket!

At the next col it was already almost four o'clock in the afternoon and time to stop the traverse: I went down a slope that wasn't too steep, on the Swiss side. Once at the bottom of a side valley, the snow became shallower, but it still took me more than three hours to reach the road between the Val Müstair and the Umbrail Pass – by then it was already dark! Sally was waiting patiently at Gasthaus Alpenrose lower down. A day of just under 11 hours of effort, stops not included.

The next day it was sunny all day. I wanted to reach Piz Chavalatsch, the last peak before Müstair, starting a little above the Gasthaus Alpenrose, to take a path of about 8 km between 2300 to 2400 m altitude. In summer, I would do it in 2-3 hours. But with 30-40 cm of snow . . .

With the learning experience of yesterday, I went to a sports shop and rented snowshoes for 2 days. This gave me a late start, and the snow was already soft. In addition, the path was not easy to find once I was above the forest. As a result,

I needed more than 3 hours for the first 3 km of the traverse, wading in the snow, and sinking in up to the ankles and further, even with snowshoes!

Finally I gave up the exercise and tried to find a way down to Müstair before dark; I had done barely half the distance to Piz Chavalatsch.

Piz Chavalatsch – still far away!

The next day (already October 24th) was again beautifully sunny. Starting from a pasture a little above Müstair, this time I managed to traverse over Piz Chavalatsch, an important summit for my circuit since it is the easternmost point of Switzerland! I arrived at the top quite quickly, again using the snowshoes. The two previous days, I had met no other person during my hike, today just two people at the top; they had come up by another route from a mountain hut on the Italian side.

View from Piz Chavalatsch down to the Müstair valley

Sally and I spent a second night at Chasa Chalavaina in Müstair, a former stagecoach stop. Then, on October 25th (and the end of summer time) we went home for a week of babysitting, a long-term commitment that had been arranged some time ago.

The last week

I was nevertheless determined to reach the river Inn in the Lower Engadine and Samnaun this year. So Sally and I went to Val Müstair for another week, taking care to bring my snowshoes. On November 2nd it was fine and sunny. The good weather of recent days had removed much of the snow on the south-facing slopes up to about 2600 m. On the slopes facing north, it was another story . . .

I left directly from the hotel and followed well marked paths to the top of Piz Terza (or Urtirolaspitz). The larches were beautiful, of a lovely yellow and golden colour, and the forest tracks very pleasant, soft under the feet because of the millions of fallen larch needles. The last 45 minutes or so were on snow and would have been more tedious if there had not been tracks left by a group of 4 or 5 people the previous day. Summit at noon. Beautiful 360° view.

The ridge to the north required snowshoes. A series of rocky outcrops covered with snow forced me to go round them on the Swiss side. The peaks after Fuorcla Starlex (col) were not possible because of the snow. I had to go down into the valley on the Italian side. This descent was uneventful, but a communication problem meant that I had to walk a few kilometres further than planned on the road. In the fairly steep-sided valleys, there was often no mobile network signal. Finally, Sally found me and took me back to the hotel.

Communication was even worse, if not disastrous, the next day. We had changed the telephone company and the previous operator cut the service for Sally, having forgotten to extend the contract for another month. I started around 9 a.m. in the Schlinig Valley. After an hour's hiking I came to the Sesvenna Hut. This mountain hut closed on October 25th, but the warden was there, ferrying up provisions on a cable car for goods. He was interested in my plans for the day but advised against the route and the ridge to the north that I had intended, because it would be too icy and I did not have any crampons with me, only snowshoes. Instead, he advised me to cross another col from the Swiss side into Italy and continue to Reschen (Resia) further on. I immediately tried to contact Sally, who was visiting Merano by train that day, by phone and SMS, to tell her where I was supposed to arrive, but there was no answer. I tried several more times during the day, without success.

The recommended path was good and signposted, but I lost my way twice where the snow had covered the marks. Again, the path was indicated neither on the Swiss national 1:25'000 map dating from 2011, nor on my GPS. Sally saw that her mobile phone was not working and did not know what to do. In the end she was saved by two very nice Italians, who ran a restaurant and pizzeria close to Sent in the Lower Engadine, where we had booked accommodation. One of them called me on his mobile phone and we fixed a meeting place for Sally in Reschen. I still had half an hour to get to this village, arriving after dark, and Sally had to drive back to pick me up. All's well that ends well! Later we ate pizzas in the restaurant of the two Italians, as a way of thanking them.

[Here I insert what Sally wrote on the last part of the day.]

And then the trouble starts. My phone is not working due to change over from Sunrise to Swisscom. I had understood that I should meet Rupert at the bridge over the Inn at 17.30. From midday he had been trying to contact me unsuccessfully. So now it is 17.30 and totally dark and I am parked where the steep and narrow road leads down to the bridge. Deserted. No contact on the phone. What to do? I go into the Pizzeria which is luckily very nearby. 'I have lost my husband'. They use their phone and get him. Marvellous. I should go back to Reschen Pass. Oh. Phew. In the dark, back to Martina, hairpin bends to Nauders, up to Pass. The Italians have fixed that we should meet at the Raffeisen Bank. I can't find it so ask in another pizzeria. Irene, she too is very kind and says the bank is in the 'Dorf' 2 km further on and there in the dark and gloom is Rupert in his black anorak. Ouf. Big hug. We go all the way back down again and stop for a pizza and thanks to the Italians. Quite a day!

I still had to ascend Piz Lad, the last peak on the Italian border, and the tripoint (Dreiländerpunkt) Switzerland-Italy-Austria which is on its northern flank. The weather was nice in the morning and the summit was not a problem.

View from Piz Lad of Reschensee

Finding the tripoint was harder because of the snow. I took a shortcut to get there faster – a steep snowy traverse – fortunately there were faint tracks of someone who had gone that way a few days previously! There is no frontier stone – the surveyors used a large limestone boulder that was more or less in the right place.

Tripoint Switzerland-Austria-Italy

This stage marked the end of the border with Italy, with its 744 km the longest border between Switzerland and a neighbouring country. Along these 744 km there was the highest point and the lowest point of the Swiss frontier (Grenzgipfel, 4632 m and Lago Maggiore, 193 m), the southernmost point and the most easterly point, as well as every 4000-metre peak!

On November 5th we left Sent quite early and were soon at the border crossing at Martina (Martinsbruck). It is from here that the frontier follows the Inn for about 6 kilometres, including a quite difficult or even impassable section in a kayak. I could have done it in the summer and with a companion, but I had also heard that the river was closed to kayakers because of a construction site. A customs officer confirmed that kayaking was indeed banned downstream from Martina this year, precisely because of the construction site. I was happy with this confirmation because, to tell the truth, I had already abandoned the idea of kayaking down the Inn – it was too late in the season, with the water too cold, and I had no companion ready to do it with me. So I did the next kilometres by bicycle.

Incidentally, it was here in Martina that I spoke to a frontier official for the first time since leaving Basel! He only came out of his office to tell us that we could not park the car here (the area was big enough and tarred, next to the river). I explained that I would be gone as soon as I had finished assembling the bicycle (I had taken off the wheels to fit the bicycle into the car). At all the other customs posts, from Basel to this point, I had seen almost no customs officers or border guards, only on very rare occasions, on main roads (e.g. at Gondo), where they were sitting in their huts or watching cars entering Switzerland.

In the end I was able to leave Martina at 9 o'clock, still in the shade, and at -2°C, to pedal 7.5 km to the Austrian border, from where I had to return a little to take the mountain road to Samnaun. I had a lot of trouble here and was often out of breath, and had to push the bicycle from time to time. There were two big road works with one-way traffic and a number of tunnels, in which I had to be careful because I did not have lights on the bicycle and was wearing a black jacket! Sally even phoned me to tell me she was worried. She was waiting for me at the first duty free market, for a coffee with Apfelstrudel, and then I had enough strength for the last 2 km up to the turn-off at Spiss (Austrian customs post).

Then I disassembled the bicycle to put it in the car, and we went on a few more kilometres to the village of Samnaun, where we found accommodation (about 70% of the hotels, inns and lodgings were already closed until the end of November). I was still too exhausted to continue hiking in the afternoon.

The next day I intended to cover the border north of Samnaun, starting from the Alp Trida. The road up there required permission from the Municipality of Compatsch, which took some time. It was therefore another late start. The road was unpaved and steep in places. Sally was very scared when she came back down and swore she would never do such roads again. She even went on strike and refused to go back to pick me up at the end of the day. So I had to plan extra time to be able to descend into the valley before dark. Everything went well, the only problem was finding the right path when most of the red and white markings were hidden under the snow on the paths. Once again, I did not see anybody all day, except 2-3 workers who were checking the ski lifts to be ready for the ski season.

I knew that Saturday, November 7th, would be the last day of my circuit for this year. We had booked accommodation in Sent in the Lower Engadine, which is very far from Samnaun. The day was planned as a tour de force to leave the Samnaun Duty Free Zone. In summer, the obvious destination would have been the Heidelberger mountain hut, but it had already closed at the end of September. To return to the Lower Engadine I had to cross the Fimber Pass (Cuolmen d'Fenga) with a long trek down the Sinestra valley down to Sent. And to get to Fimber pass from Samnaun I had to cross two other passes, the Zeblasjoch and the Fuorcla Val Gronda.

Leaving Samnaun

Fuorcla Val Gronda

It was a beautiful sunny day. All went well, but the section between the Zeblas Pass and the Fimber Pass and beyond, even going down to the level of the Heidelberger hut, required snowshoes and was very laborious in the soft snow and in the absence of clearly visible trails. In addition, bands of grass and rubble forced me to remove the snowshoes (and to put them back on again) some eight or nine times in all. Sally once again had a problem finding the beginning of the right forest road above Sent, which caused some phone calls, and it was already dark when I emerged from the forest where she was waiting.

The next peaks on the Austrian border, starting with the Fluchthorn, could not reasonably be done in 2015 – there was too much snow, I needed a guide or a partner, the mountain huts were closed (until the ski touring season), and the days were too short. These summits, and the rest of the border circuit, would probably have to wait until July 2016.

For this day, I put the following text at the end of the daily blog.

It has been a great adventure so far! People have asked me how many kilometres I have done, how much I have climbed, etc. So here are some statistics (I am grateful to my brother Rolf who started compiling the figures in a table on a daily basis).

Days involved: 98, including 5 rest days but not travel days
Kilometres covered: 1784, of which 137 by bicycle and 88 by kayak
Hours walked, cycled and by kayak, total: 625
Vertical distances: uphill 102'660 metres, downhill 105'650 metres
Kilometres of frontier covered: 1358 (France 572, Italy 744, Austria 42)

The Grisons, third part

Fuorcla Val Gronda (Samnaun) – the Rhine near Sargans

The programme for 2016

After the stop in November 2015, it was essential to continue the tour – and finish it – as soon as possible in 2016. I had the idea that I could cross the Silvretta range on skis, touring with skins. The month of March was foreseen for this escapade and I had recruited my daughter Sonia and two friends to do it. I had even booked the mountain huts, already in January because the area is very popular among ski tourists. Unfortunately I had to give up the idea, being sick again and stuck in hospital during this time. The others, however, were able to go, taking advantage of the bookings, but the unstable weather allowed them to reach only one summit on the border. I had planned holidays elsewhere in April. Another opportunity would have been in May but the weather was still bad.

It was then necessary to wait for the summer. In mid-June, after weeks of bad weather, having followed the snow conditions on several webcams, I saw that there was still too much snow in the mountains and floods in many valleys. So I decided to take up the circuit on the Liechtenstein-Switzerland border on the Rhine near Sargans and continue to the canton of Schaffhausen, returning to the mountains later. That section will be the subject of a later chapter.

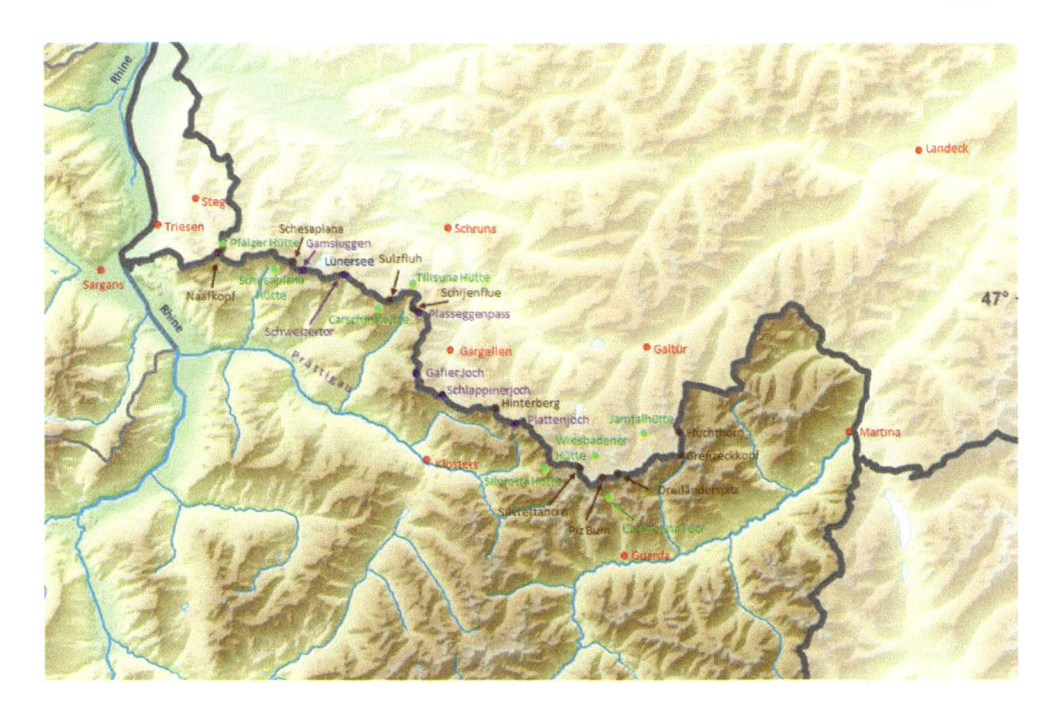

Back in the mountains

It was not too difficult to start again in the mountains of the Silvretta range, you just had to take out all the mountaineering equipment, starting with the boots, and prepare the maps and the guidebooks. My daughter Sonia wanted to spend a few days with me. I managed to find a mountain guide in Davos for 3-4 days. While talking to him, I learned that the Fluchthorn would not be advisable for a while because of the snow. We agreed to meet at the Chamonna (= hut) Tuoi above Guarda in the Lower Engadine on the evening of June 30th.

I drove with Sonia to Galtür in Austria and climbed up to the Jamtal Hut two days before that date. The hut had been open for only a few days and was almost empty – 25 people that night, for 182 beds. "What a contrast with the month of March!" said Sonia, who had been there on her ski trip.

From there we went up to a col and then to a summit called Grenzeckkopf before going down to the hut by another way. It was not difficult, but we took all the gear with us, "just in case", and our rucksacks were a little too heavy, which was good training. There was a fair amount of snow and we sank in up to our hips in the soft snow in places (it had not frozen during the night). We had finally to give up trying the Fluchthorn, the highest peak in the region with its 3398 m in height;

the hut warden confirmed that the conditions were not suitable and no one had yet tried it this year.

After the Grenzeckkopf

Reaching the Chamonna Tuoi from the Jamtal requires crossing the mountain range over a col located at approximately 3060 m. We had to abandon this idea – unfamiliar terrain (for us), poor visibility due to fog, no tracks in the snow and the forecast of rain – the decision was then quickly taken to go down to Galtür and drive around to Guarda, via Landeck and Martina. The day was rainy and we were lucky to be able to hike from Guarda to the hut and to get there just before the next downpour. The very young guide David Hefti arrived in the evening. We were the only visitors in the hut!

Dreiländerspitz and Piz Buin

The forecast for July 1st was good – it was correct! There were only a few clouds and a beautiful sea of fog in the valley. We left for the Dreiländerspitz, 3197 m, which is climbed from the north on a snowy glacier and a steeper snow slope, then on a not too difficult rocky ridge. We were at the top at 10 a.m. and at the

Wiesbadenerhütte in Austria at noon. One of the advantages of a guide is that you do not waste time finding the way and looking at the map and the GPS! In fact, the snow conditions were good, there were tracks and we did not need to put on crampons. A very nice excursion, completed successfully!

Going up the Dreiländerspitz

Summit marker

The Dreiländerspitz is the tripoint shared by the three "countries" of the Grisons, Vorarlberg and Tyrol. It lies on the watershed between the Rhine and the Danube.

Then it was the Piz Buin, 3312 m, whose name is well known to users of sun cream. We learned that the first ascent took place on July 14th, 1865, exactly the same day as the first ascent of the Matterhorn! We arrived at the summit without mishap, in overcast and windy weather, with no view because of the cloud. The ascent itself was quite easy, but the approach on soft snow covering the glaciers was quite tedious, as was the 4-5 km traverse to the Silvretta Hut, for which David had to make the track.

Piz Buin, on the right

With Sonia and David Hefti on the summit

For Sonia, this day marked the end of her days off; she left the hut early in the afternoon to catch a bus to Klosters and go home. David and I greatly enjoyed her company.

Another 4 peaks

For his third day with me David gave me 2-3 options. I chose to cross four peaks along the border to the northwest of Piz Buin – Signalhorn, Egghorn, Silvrettahorn and Rotflue, which surround the upper Silvretta glacier, with all the connecting ridges. It turned into a fantastic day of 8-9 hours. The weather was fine after some morning fog, giving us great views all the rest of the day. It was also a varied circuit – steep slopes, snow-capped peaks, some interesting but easy rock climbing. The only "negative" point, our mountain boots had not dried out overnight and thanks to the wet snow we had wet feet all day.

David returned home in the afternoon, leaving me alone for another night in the hut. The weather forecast was good for the next day. I would have liked to climb another summit on the border, but there was no guide available and, as I saw later, any ascent would have been very difficult because of the amount of snow still in the mountains and on the approach walks. In fact, there was (soft) snow everywhere above 2400 m, except on south-facing slopes.

So I went instead to the Plattenjoch, on the border, through a connecting pass 400 metres from the border called "Scharte" (small col) – a very original name! I did it without any problem – there were even very old barely visible tracks that made my route-finding easier. There followed a leisurely walk down into the valley, from where a minibus (cheap at 4.45 p.m., if reserved) took me to Klosters for a train to Guarda, where I was able to pick up the car and find accommodation. I called my blog of that day "A day of relaxation?", but there were still more than 7 hours of walking!

Schlappin – a Walser village

The next day was a day off: I took the car from Guarda to Schlappin (north of Klosters Dorf) via the Flüelapass. I had finished with the Engadine. The small hamlet of Schlappin has several farms and houses in the Walser style and two inns, including the very nice and friendly Berggasthaus Erika, where I stayed. I received a message from Christoph Brändle from Basel, who had accompanied me the previous year on the second day of my trip, telling me that he wanted to do another 3-4 days with me. I accepted with pleasure and arranged to meet him the next evening at Klosters Dorf station. He had spent several weeks in New Zealand where he was able to do many hikes.

Schlappin

While waiting for him, I aimed at a col on the border and Hinterberg, one of the only summits in the region that I could do safely. All other peaks were either too rocky or only accessible through steep snow slopes. My trip started with some 6 km on an unpaved agricultural road in the valley. Not wanting to do them in mountain boots, I walked in trainers and put the boots and spare socks in my backpack. In the end this worked out well – the trainers got wet in a grassy meadow and I could put on dry socks with the boots at the col. The Hinterberg was climbing on steep grass and scree from the south.

I was able to go down the other side of the Hinterberg and join a trail quite close to the border. This trail took me back to the border at Schlappinerjoch, from where I could go back down to Schlappin. This descent did not give me much pleasure – the path was undergoing an "improvement", that is to say a widening to convert it into a track suitable for mountain bikes, in fact a small road about 3 metres wide, bare earth, with round wooden logs every 10-15 metres to lead rainwater away. The whole construction did not look nice; maybe it would be better in 2-3 years when the vegetation will have grown back again. I asked a couple of mountain bikers who were on their way down (and I was able to overtake) what they thought. They were not happy at all, having to get off the bike at almost every log! The owner of the Berggasthaus, however, said it was a good thing – a development that would attract more bikers and allow competitions.

An "improved" footpath!   Christoph

Christoph came from Basel to Klosters Dorf by train and I went down to collect him before supper. A happy reunion! He had not changed since last year, except for longer hair and a small beard. He is always very fit and always keen to do a little bit extra.

Two days with Christoph

On July 7th it was sunny all day. We left with the lightest rucksacks possible and soon reached the Prättigauer high level path. This took us round to the north close to the border which we hit again after a steep climb to the Gafier Joch. On the way we noticed many interesting mushrooms growing out of dried-out cowpats. They are well known for being hallucinogenic. We did not try!

Psilocybe sp.

From the Gafier Joch an easy descent led us to the upper station of the Gargellen cable car, where we had a well-deserved beer! I had booked rooms in Gargellen in the Austrian Montafon, but had to pick up the car again. Christoph was ready to accompany me – down into the valley and crossing back to Schlappin via the Schlappinerjoch, all in sweltering heat. Christoph found that the sole of one of his boots was starting to come off: after a makeshift repair with laces he managed to finish the crossing. At the sight of the pretty little lake in front of the Berggasthaus Erika he could not resist swimming for a few seconds (the temperature was maybe 8°C!).

Later we left by car and went to a commercial centre near Sargans where a not too enthusiastic "Mister Minit" managed to glue the sole on again (for how long?) Finally we arrived at the village of Gargellen in time for dinner.

The next day we started somewhat late after a good breakfast and the cable car ride. We climbed back up to the Gafier Joch, then along the ridge to the north on marked trails. Further on it was necessary to go down more than 500 m in height before being able to go up to the Plasseggenpass, then to go round the amazing calcareous rock formations of the Schijenflue, with quite a lot of small climbs and descents, before reaching the Tilisuna Hut for a soup and a beer.

We left this hut at 3 p.m. for the summit of the Sulzfluh, walking first on slabs and limestone scree, and finally on snow, leaving our rucksacks about 20 minutes before the summit. We were the last ones on the summit that day. We then ran down steep snow couloirs and scree – Christoph said it was the most pleasant and least tiring descent he had ever experienced! The sole of his freshly glued shoe had held well all day. At the end, we crossed under the imposing south face of the Sulzfluh to the Carschina Hut, where we once again arrived just before supper time.

It rained during the night and in the morning the weather was still very gloomy, with many clouds hiding all the summits. The path was still very wet and there were black salamanders everywhere, walking along the path, watching from small pebbles, sometimes mating.

Black salamander

We were soon at the col named Schweizertor and continued towards the Lünersee, an artificial lake behind a dam. The weather took its time to improve and we met the first hikers. But impossible to climb any peaks.

Alphorns

At the Lünersee it was already fairly sunny. We heard alphorns on the other side of the lake, which we skirted to the west. There was a small crowd at a refreshment bar – two Swiss were giving an alphorn concert. Further on along the way, we met yet more groups of musicians. We learned that there was an alphorn festival, with maybe sixty different groups, from Switzerland and Austria, each group with 3-6 players. Many of these groups were walking round the lake, stopping along the way and playing for a few minutes before going on further, and the tunes could be heard from all around the lake. Amazing party atmosphere! Besides, I did not know that alphorns were played also in Austria, at least in Vorarlberg.

At the Douglass Hut, where the Lünersee cable car ends, there were many people eating, drinking and taking pictures of the musicians – we did the same!

Alphorn festival around the Lünersee

I had fixed to meet Sally and my (half) brother Walter at Schruns that evening. So we went down on foot almost to the main valley, where it was very hot. We took a break at a bus stop; Christoph looked at the timetable and discovered that there was one due to arrive within 5 minutes, the service only starting today! And already the little bus was there; we found room in it to go down the last kilometre to the railway station. 40 minutes later we took the next train to Schruns, 4-5 km further on, where we were greeted by Sally. With her, I took the bus to Gargellen to pick up the car. Finally, we settled down in a hotel (shower, pool and sauna for some) and had a good meal with Christoph and Walter.

Christoph, myself, Sally, Walter

Christoph went home the next day and Walter took his place, so to speak, for the end of the mountain journey, that is to say until we reached the Rhine opposite Sargans. Walter had already wanted to do one or two stages with me last year but the timing never worked out because of the time I lost. We tried again this year and I was happy that we were able to find not only suitable dates but also interesting and not too difficult stages.

Sally drove Walter and myself to the Lünersee cable car. The car park was crowded – it was Sunday and it was sunny – she could not park the car close enough and so she went back down to the next village, where she could still see and listen to the alphorn players.

The rest of the blog for this day:

"From the upper station, Walter and I went up to the Totalp Hut for a drink, then to the Schesaplana, no problem, except for two small sections of somewhat steep snow. Beautiful views from the summit. At the descent we branch off on the well signposted but snowy path leading to the Gamsluggen. A few chains facilitate this rather tricky passage. Finally we follow the Prättigauer Höhenweg to the Schesaplana Hut where there is a good atmosphere. We eat outside under the setting sun – magnificent "

Totalp Hut, Sunday lunchtime

Walter at the Gamsluggen

On July 11th the weather was still fine. The day looked pretty easy. From the Schesaplana Hut we progressed nicely on well-marked paths to the Pfälzerhütte. We had to cross countless snow-covered fields and ravines on the last section, including one quite steep gully. After checking in for the night at the hut we climbed the Naafkopf, without our backpacks. The view was once again splendid. Three Dutch hikers arrived after us at the top – in fact we had overtaken them lower down. They were looking for a geo-cache, but I don't know if they found it.

The Pfälzerhütte in Liechtenstein

The Naafkopf is the highest mountain in Liechtenstein, albeit shared, as it is also the point where Austria, Liechtenstein and Switzerland meet. The Pfälzerhütte is one of only two mountain huts in Liechtenstein. It lies right inside the border with Austria – looking at the frontier stones next to the hut it seemed to me that the border had been moved by 2-3 metres to facilitate the construction!

The weather forecast for the next day was very bad. It rained a lot during the night. In the morning, it was not raining anymore but the sky was overcast, with many clouds hiding the peaks. We then decided to descend to the Rhine as soon as possible by a more direct route. After 2 hours of walking, we arrived at a small inn where we were hoping for at least a coffee. But a sign indicated that they were closed that day because of mourning. The inn overlooks Steg, an interesting village – houses and barns all around a large rectangle of meadows and cultivated fields, the signature of a Walser-founded village.

A short tunnel took us to the slopes above Triesenberg, from where we had our first view of the Rhine in the mist 1000 metres below. The end was now not very far! It was colder and there was still a little fog. A good path led to Triesenberg where we got lost among the villas and the paths of a Vita trail. It began to rain slightly and we found the main road that descends to Triesen in hairpin bends (no shortcuts, no paths found, neither on the map nor on the ground). It was raining harder and harder and soon we were in a very heavy downpour. Sally phoned me from the valley below where she had just arrived and I asked her to pick us up. Finally, we arrived at the first houses of Triesen and could shelter under trees, where Sally found us, completely soaked, about 500 m from the Rhine. We went to an inn for a snack and to dry ourselves out.

First view of the Rhine at Sargans

This stage marked the end of the mountainous section between Samnaun and the Rhine (Silvretta and Rätikon ranges). This new situation took a little time to sink into my mind. I found that I was both happy and sad – very happy, because this part was over and I was closer to accomplishing my goal and my dream, but also sad because there would be no more mountain trails, no more peace and loneliness along the way and I would also miss the atmosphere of the mountain huts and the human contacts with the people I met.

Mountain guides

A short quiz:

They go slightly too fast, they do not stop often enough, so you do not have time to take pictures.

From a mountain hut in the early morning, they go too fast on scree and stony paths and let you stumble because you do not find the best way in the dark.

When you go down snowfields, they let you go in front, then they criticise you because you don't go exactly where they want or because you are following a bad track.

Each one ropes up a little differently and tells you off because you applied what the last one taught you.

Who are they?

You guessed right – mountain guides!

Well, that was a somewhat humorous, slightly exaggerated impression of their behaviour that I experienced, but there is some truth behind it. What I felt most was that it bothered me to ask for a short stop to take photos.

In fact, I had 8 different guides. All were very professional and competent, very concerned about my safety and quite cautious. If there were doubts about my skills, my fitness or my age, I did not see anything! It must be difficult to start a climb with someone you don't know (but that's the guide's profession!) Anyway, each one was friendly and I always felt comfortable with them.

In the Valais, I had 5 different guides, organised by the Frost Guiding office in Evolène, in fact Graham Frost and his wife Janine. They made a big effort to explain my project to the guides, so that they understood what I wanted. They found good guides, all of English or Scottish origin, based in the Chamonix region or in the Valais. They were very familiar with the classic routes and the Haute Route, but they had to improvise a bit as soon as they came off the beaten track – I sometimes thought that a local guide would have found the way better. But in the end I was very happy with the arrangement, which saved me from having to look for the guides directly myself. These were the following guides:

Victor Saunders – the only one who did a prior reconnaissance; he did not hesitate to consult the map in a region he did not know well. It was he who sold me the idea of only climbing the most important summits rather than each gendarme or intermediate peak in a mountain range.

Graham Frost – the "veteran"; I felt his experience and his vast knowledge of the region. A good companion.

Dave Green – a good connoisseur of the area but perhaps too cautious and more critical. He had clearly discussed various routes with Graham and received his instructions. A great shame he was unable to do the Matterhorn with me because of a foot injury.

Euan Whittaker – very enthusiastic. He carried a small camera and took a lot of pictures, many of which I was able to use.

Dave Kenyon – very flexible, ready to improvise, to accept long days and get to places he did not know. His speciality: he did not like to go down too much and lose altitude, which is very understandable, hence the tendency to take shortcuts that sometimes proved bad or a waste of time.

For the other three:

Giorgio Cazzanelli on the Matterhorn was excellent because he knew the route inside out. He had his routine and knew exactly where to rope up, for example. It was the Guides' Office in Cervinia that found him for me quite quickly and at very short notice.

Lukas Mathis (Cima di Castello and Monte del Forno in the Bernina range) guided me well, led me through crevasses and improvised on routes he had possibly never done before. He also asked for my opinion on possible variants. It was the Pontresina Guides' Office that found him for me. This office had given me very valuable advice, especially on snow conditions.

David Hefti (Silvretta range), very young and enthusiastic, took a lot of pictures and I think he was delighted with the superb conditions. He was also ready to do a special day with me that included a summit he probably did not know yet. He trusted me and my daughter Sonia; at the Dreiländerspitz, we climbed together with few belays and were therefore quite fast. He was hired through the Pontresina Guides' Office, via Davos.

There are pictures of all of them on my website.

The Upper Rhine, Lake Constance and Schaffhausen

Sargans – Nohl

The Upper Rhine in flood

The month of June 2016 was very rainy; there was a lot of flooding everywhere, but especially in the Grisons and Ticino valleys. Despite these somewhat unfavourable conditions, I wanted to restart my border circuit as soon as possible.

I left for Sargans on June 19th, 2016 with Sally (transport and logistics) and our son Roger, who was kind enough to accompany me for 2 days, either by kayak or by bicycle. We had the two-seater kayak and 2 bicycles on the car. In gloomy and rainy weather, we did a reconnaissance near Buchs and further downstream. The water level was quite high and the current very fast, with some eddies and standing waves below the bridge piers. It was feasible in a kayak but it was safer to choose the bicycle. So it was decided!

The next day we started cycling where the border with Liechtenstein joins the Rhine. The weather was still dull, with a few drops of rain, but it improved as we moved north.

Between the Rhine at Altstätten and Lake Constance there is only a height difference of about twenty metres for a distance of some 18 km. Originally, the river did not flow due north but passed east of Diepoldsau before making a pronounced bend to the west at St. Margrethen. Because of the low slope, alluvium transported by the Alpine Rhine was deposited and raised the riverbed. In order to put an end to the catastrophic floods of the nineteenth century, a correction of the river channel was undertaken in the years 1896 to 1923, consisting in damming the river and leading it straight to the lake, that is to say by accentuating the slope. The border however remained the same along the Old Rhine (Alter Rhein), so that when the construction work was finished Diepoldsau had moved from the west to the east of the river!

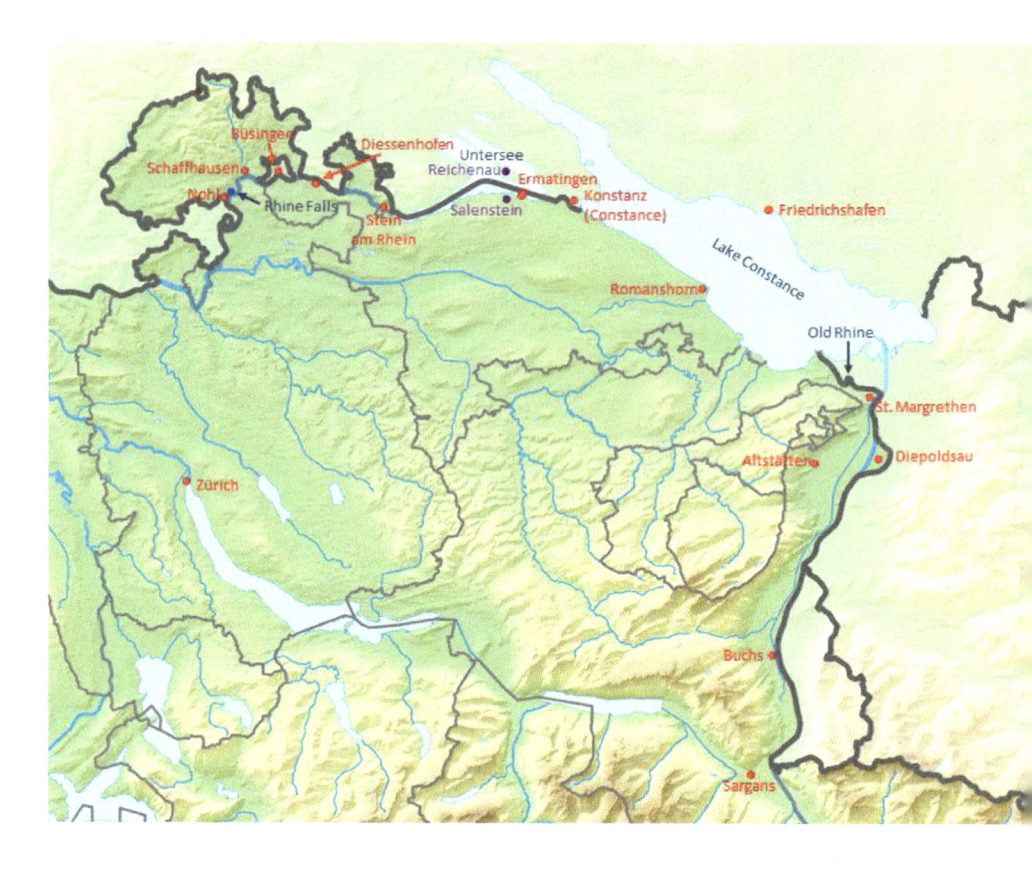

The Upper Rhine, view looking
north towards Sargans

The bicycle trail along the Rhine was very straightforward and pleasant, mostly tarred. The water level must have been 2-3 metres higher two days earlier; there was a lot of wood (tree trunks, etc.) on the embankments.

Wood left on the Rhine two days earlier,
view kooking south

Start on the Old Rhine

Well before midday, we met Sally near St. Margrethen and exchanged the bicycles for the kayak to descend the Old Rhine. There was enough current the first kilometres, then we had to paddle. We had to make our way through branches at a place where a tree had fallen over the river, making a "dam" with other debris.

A serious obstacle!

The triangle between the canalised Rhine, the Old Rhine and Lake Constance forms the Rhine freshwater delta (as opposed to the large sea delta in the Netherlands). A nature reserve of more than 2000 hectares was created in 1982 after years of negotiations. The reserve serves as a refuge for over 330 bird species, making it a natural site of international importance.

The Rhine delta in Lake Constance

Lake Constance

Arriving at the mouth of the Old Rhine (where there is a large marina), we headed directly to Romanshorn, another fifteen kilometres away, where we already enjoyed good weather. This town is linked several times a day to Friedrichshafen in Germany across Lake Constance, by means of 2 ferries, MF Romanshorn and MF Euregia (MF: MotorFähre). The ferry link, created in 1929, was also used to transport railroad cars until 1976.

When these ferry boats leave the port, their status becomes uncertain since they enter a kind of legal no man's land, the border on the lake between Switzerland and Germany having never been defined in a treaty. In fact, the national borders have been unclear ever since the Treaties of Westphalia in 1648 and the definitive (*de jure*) recognition of the independence of the Swiss Confederation. This uncertainty seems to bother only a few professors of international law . . .

Floods on the banks of the Untersee

The next day the weather was once again overcast and dull but without rain. My right shoulder was hurting, so I did not want to commit to another 45 km kayaking. I went by bicycle with Roger, following the pedestrian path that was closest to the lake (but sometimes forbidden for bicycles!). The official bicycle trail often went too far from the lake and was less interesting. The water level in the lake being quite high, there were some flooded sections to cross. Arriving at the Rhine on the west side of the town of Constance, already on the part called the Untersee, we found the fields flooded and chose not to kayak the next section, especially with the wind coming from the northwest (i.e. a headwind for us). So we decided to continue cycling to Ermatingen.

Opposite Ermatingen, a few hundred metres from the border, there is the German island of Reichenau, which was connected to the mainland by a dike in 1838. The island with its abbey, founded in 724 AD by St. Pirmin, has been listed as a Unesco World Heritage Site since the year 2000. At the beginning of the 11th century, Reichenau was a renowned school of manuscripts that produced the most beautiful illuminations, such as those of the Codex Egberti.

Illumination in the Codex Egberti (City of Trier library)

Just opposite the island, a little further west on the Swiss bank, there is Salenstein and the castle Arenenberg where prince Louis Napoleon, the future Napoleon III, resided. A Napoleon Museum and extensive gardens of 13 hectares can be visited. See https://napoleonmuseum.tg.ch/en.html/7107.

The level of the Untersee was 70-80 cm higher than normal: the footpath was often flooded up to about 40 cm, great fun to cycle through, shoes and trousers getting wet or soaked.

Public beach

In Ermatingen we exchanged the bicycles for the kayak. Several roads near the lake were flooded and closed to traffic, as was the entire car park next to the pier. We continued in the kayak for the section up to the border between Stein am Rhein and Öhningen (D); this was quite laborious due to the headwind. We "celebrated" with a good dinner in Stein am Rhein as a farewell to Roger who was going to leave us the next day.

Car park at Ermatingen

On June 22nd I left the customs post Stein am Rhein – Öhningen (D) on foot. I covered the eastern part of the canton of Schaffhausen, on the right bank of the Rhine, which includes several villages as well as Stein am Rhein itself. My blog for this day said:

"Sunny and warm. Alternation of forests and cultivated fields. In the forests the only good tracks were marked and generally led from one village or farm to another, but did not usually follow the border, which gave route-finding problems and adventures in undergrowth and swampy areas.

In the fields, one had to keep to small agricultural roads, which gave a lot of tedious zigzags to stay near the border, which moreover often passed through cultivated fields. Many tractors at work, with farmers taking advantage of the sun. "

After 34 km and 7½ hours of walking I was back at the Rhine, which I then followed for 3-4 km to the bridge in Diessenhofen to find Sally.

Muddy paths around the canton of Schaffhausen

The canton of Schaffhausen, almost entirely on the right bank Rhine, has a "meandering" border of more than 150 km with Germany. In many places the trace defies all logic! The next day was scheduled for most of this border, this time by bicycle. I left Diessenhofen and followed small roads and forest roads along the frontier as best I could, with many ups and downs to the main goal of the day, the northernmost point of Switzerland, a place named Schwarze Staa (= Schwarzer Stein). Here there was a frontier stone, an information board and some picnic tables, and a nice view to the south. The border led from here to a minor summit, the Hoher Randen. The subsequent descent on a forest road was quite strenuous, since the track had been churned up by tractors pulling tree trunks, making it muddy and wet, almost impassable on foot, and even more so with a bicycle on one's back . . .

Frontier stone at Schwarzer Staa   Difficult section on a bicycle!

The next day it was still nice and warm all day. I continued by bicycle, crossing three ranges of hills before reaching the Rhine at Nohl three and a half hours later, thus completing the circuit of the main part of the canton of Schaffhausen. I still had time to pedal to the German enclave of Büsingen on the other side of Schaffhausen. After about 1 km I was in the middle of hordes of tourists (cycling not permitted for 250 m) with a superb view of the Rhine Falls.

Two views of the Rhine Falls

It took 8-9 km along the Rhine on very pleasant bicycle trails and paved roads to reach the enclave, the circuit of which took about an hour and a half. Then I crossed Schaffhausen on major roads to join Sally in the outskirts, which saved her from having to go through the city, where the late afternoon traffic was frightful.

For the record: most of the frontier stones around Schaffhausen date from 1839. They are marked CS on the Swiss side (= Canton Schaffhausen) and GB on the other side. Later I found the solution to this enigma: GB means Großherzogtum Baden (Grand Duchy of Baden), a state apparently created by Napoleon. But it was only in 1839 that the boundary was formally defined.

The history of the city of Schaffhausen includes a very sad event. On Saturday, April 1st, 1944 at the time of the market, a US squadron dropped hundreds of incendiary and explosive bombs on the city, killing dozens of people and causing great damage. Navigation error or retaliation? It will probably never be known. Following the apology of President Franklin Roosevelt, the US Government paid Switzerland more than 62 million francs in 1949 as compensation for the loss of life and destruction in 1944 following bombings of Schaffhausen, as well as of Zurich and Basel.

From Schaffhausen to Basel

Nohl to Basel

Reconnaissance and timing

From Schaffhausen I needed only 4-5 days to complete my journey. I could have done it the following week. But I had to carry out a reconnaissance along the Rhine downstream from Schaffhausen. There are about 7-8 dams and power plants on this stretch of the river and we had to decide where we could launch the kayak and take it out again. The first thing was to look at these dams from the point of view of access, possible prohibitions and dangers, especially below the dams. It was also necessary to see which sections could or should be done by bicycle. Moreover, my daughter Sonia had long ago fixed the day of her (second) wedding for July 23rd, in Scotland. To finish before this date seemed a little tight.

We had also planned a small party in Basel at the end of my circuit, more precisely at the Dreiländereck. Sonia wanted her two sons, Natan and Neil, to attend the party and she set Saturday August 6th for this event. So I had enough time to finish without being in a hurry, even though I was a bit frustrated by the additional delay. In the end neither Natan nor Neil came that day, for various reasons!

A "circuit" of 12 hours

Located 1 km from the frontier, the Rhine Falls are impressive, especially during high water. The stages of their origin about 17,000 to 14,000 years ago (that is very recently, geologically speaking) are well established. They are the direct consequence of successive glaciations. The waterfall is where a bed of Jurassic limestone, a harder stone (upstream), gives way to a bed of sediment or more friable rock (downstream).

Another view of the Rhine Falls

After these falls, there is a stretch of border on the Rhine, then a sizeable piece of Swiss territory north of the Rhine known as the Rafzerfeld – which is mainly part of the canton of Zurich, but also a small enclave of the canton of Schaffhausen – which starts in front of Ellikon am Rhein and ends upstream of the Eglisau power plant in Rheinsfelden. (Not to be confused with Rheinfelden, a town on the river further downstream.) From then on, the border lies in the middle of the Rhine all the way to Basel.

The reconnaissance showed that it would be very difficult to access the river, both by boat and by car, where the frontier meets the river about 1½ km downstream from Nohl (and 2½ km downstream from the Rhine Falls). The bank is very steep and forested, almost impenetrable with a kayak. In addition, there are 3 dams, all requiring portage of the kayak, around the "loop" of Rheinau, known for its abbey on an island in the middle of the Rhine. So this was a section to do by bicycle.

Rheinau abbey

To do this stretch, as well as the circuit of the Swiss territory north of the Rhine, I left my house by car just before 6 a.m. and reached the Eglisau train station to the north of Zürich in time to reassemble the bicycle (which was in the car with the front wheel off) and prepare my bag before taking the train to Neuhausen (near the Rhine Falls) at 08.40. From Neuhausen station I had less than 2 km to the footbridge at Nohl, the real beginning of the circuit of the day. I followed good cycle tracks on the Swiss side to Rheinau, where I crossed the Rhine to do the next part on the German side (there is no bridge in Ellikon am Rhein).

The rest of the day's tour was mostly on tracks and unpaved roads through forests or farmland, with occasional paths that were no longer there or were completely overgrown (but fortunately there were no brambles!) or very muddy and/or steep, or which led through a fenced field, all of these conditions probably slightly worse on the German side of the border. There were many climbs and descents, which I found quite exhausting. In my blog of the day I even talked about cyclocross! Finally, I arrived at the end of the day's circuit at the Eglisau

(Rheinsfelden) power plant where it's possible for pedestrians and cyclists to cross the river.

Eglisau hydroelectric plant, at Rheinsfelden

I then still had 3-4 km on a main road to reach my car at Eglisau station, from where I could return home. Total round trip for the day: just over 12 hours.

The descent of the Rhine

On August 2nd Sally and I spent the night in the small historic town of Kaiserstuhl, with the single-seater kayak on the roof of the car and bicycle in it. The next day we did the few kilometres to the hydroelectric plant in Rheinsfelden. Reaching the actual river on a very stony ramp proved a little tricky, but in the end we were able to launch the kayak and I could leave. Four kilometres away, Sally was waiting for me at the Kaiserstuhl road bridge for photos. Sally was also waiting for me at two power plants where portages of the kayak were necessary.

My descent that day was uneventful, the current varied between 2-3 km / h and a maximum of 12 km / h (speeds measured by GPS). There were a lot of small eddies where water rose to the surface, not dangerous but making it more difficult to keep a straight line. At one place a sign surprised me by announcing rapids in the next 1500 m, which I had not seen on the satellite photos. It made me a little nervous. In fact, there were higher waves but I passed this stretch without any problems. For a few kilometres I suffered from an unpleasant headwind, especially before Leibstadt, but otherwise it was a beautiful day, almost 42 km in the kayak, which gave me a lot of pleasure.

Leaving Rheinsfelden   World War II bunker

Two interesting facts: first, at the portage at the Reckingen power plant, there were 2 carts for carrying small boats, where one had to put a coin in a slot as a deposit, exactly as for the trolleys at supermarkets. We found this very convenient! Secondly, I was able to take a picture of the cooling tower of the Leibstadt nuclear power plant without the usual steam feathers or clouds above – I learned later that they had stopped operations 1-2 days earlier for a periodic inspection.

Laufenburg – interesting history and special geological situation

Historical aspects: Laufenburg, on both sides of the Rhine, had been part of the Habsburg territories since the 12th century – later referred to as Anterior Austria – until the Treaty of Lunéville in February 1801. Napoleon then decided that the Rhine should be the border of the Helvetic Republic. Laufenburg was divided in two, the southern part became part of the canton Fricktal and after the Act of Mediation in 1803 was attached to the canton of Aargau. The northern part became part of the Grand Duchy of Baden, today the German state of Baden-Württemberg.

Geographical aspects: The Rhine carved a passage through the crystalline rocks (red gneiss) of the Black Forest, which resulted in a gorge, only 12 metres wide, with rapids (a descent of 10 metres in one kilometre). The word Laufen meant fast or cascading in old German. For a long time floaters (Laufenknechte) steered the boats through the Laufen rapids, while the goods were transported in carts by land, which represented an important source of revenue for the town. Log rafts had to be disassembled before the rapids, then tied together again after the rapids.

With the construction of the dam for the Laufenburg power plant – incidentally the first one on the Rhine and the largest at the time – between 1909 and 1914, the rapids were submerged. The floater profession became obsolete. The current bridge was built in 1910.

The last stage on the Rhine

For August 4th, I planned to make a first stretch, to the hydroelectric plant Rheinfelden, by bicycle. I left Laufenburg in sunny weather. At first there were some small climbs and descents on steps on the path close to the river. Then, after the Laufenburg power plant, the path became quite flat and later turned into a good cycle track. I met one or two cyclists and a large group of walkers. At Stein AG there is the longest wooden covered bridge in Europe (we had been told the day before), about 220 m long, leading to Bad Säckingen in Germany.

Later, I was able to take advantage of good forest roads in woodland. I finally arrived at the Rheinfelden power plant where Sally was waiting for me. We prepared the kayak; the bicycle went on the car (for the last time!) The descent to Kaiseraugst was very pleasant. Here, where you could see storks on nests on some chimneys and on the church tower, there is a lock for large boats, but nothing for the small ones. I had to dock at the campsite / swimming pool, where Sally met me. Then a fairly long portage (on a paved road, with wheels under the kayak) brought us to the shore downstream of the dam of the next power plant.

Kaiseraugst is the site of a Roman stronghold, Castrum Rauracense, which succeeded the city Augusta Raurica, whose period of prosperity declined in the third century AD under the pressure of the peoples from the north. It was also the site of a bridge over the Rhine, whose remains of a beachhead can be visited on the north shore. Already then, the river played the role of a frontier. Looking at the Rhine today, very wide at this place, one wonders how the Romans could have placed pylons for a bridge in a powerful current and to a depth that one can imagine to be several metres. More likely, it was a pontoon bridge.

The site of Augusta Raurica is currently well endowed with explanatory panels in several languages. The small museum displays various objects discovered during the excavations, including a famous treasure composed of 270 silver coins. One sees many coins of incredible quality (they had never been used) and fine ceremonial objects including the beautiful Achilles platter.

The bridge crossed the Rhine
exactly here

The Achilles platter

Downstream from Kaiseraugst the last kayaking section was much less pleasant, with a strong headwind, almost no current, and many industrial installations and docks on the Swiss side (coal being unloaded, for example) and strong chemical odours.

I finished at the frontier between Grenzach and Riehen, where I landed on a platform belonging to the Basel Rowing Club (where there was nobody) and I had to heave the kayak up to the main road. Then I had to wait an hour – Sally, having made a mistake somewhere and finding herself on the wrong side of the Rhine, was stuck in the queues of the cross-border commuters. I spent my time observing Basel residents coming back from working or shopping in Germany, who stopped near the customs, ran into the German customs building to have their documents validated to recover VAT on their purchases, returned to their cars and departed in a hurry. An almost continuous performance between 5 and 6 p.m.

All that remained to be done now was the last stretch on land, the Basel-Stadt loop on the right bank of the Rhine, some 25 kilometres long.

There were logistical considerations for August 6th. Christoph Brändle wanted to accompany me this last day, as well as Urs Scholer, also from Basel, a former colleague and boss and a very good friend. Among other things, he wanted to show me the only vineyard in the canton (technically a half-canton) of Basel-Stadt, the Schlipf, north of Riehen. Then, my younger daughter Natalie wanted to hike the last segment of 5-6 km with me with her 3 children. For the first two, the meeting was arranged at the customs Riehen-Grenzacherstrasse at 8 a.m., for the others the terminus of the tram at the customs of Riehen-Lörrach at midday. Then we had to have the kayak in Kleinhüningen and all that was needed for a reception party near the Dreiländereck.

Going up the Unterberg

Around the "Eiserne Hand"

The day was beautiful and sunny but there was still morning fog in the Rhine Valley. With Christoph and Urs, I was soon in the forest climbing the Unterberg and I missed the correct path among a multitude of trails that crisscrossed in the forest, which cost us a few precious minutes. Christoph had fun taking a picture of each frontier stone – it must be said that some were very interesting. On the Swiss side, there was almost always the emblem of the bishopric of Basel, the dates being very diverse, generally between 1800 and 1900 – but the oldest was 1600 – while on the German side there was sometimes the coat of arms of the Grand Duchy of Baden, sometimes the different arms of German municipalities or lords, some of which we failed to identify.

Urs and Christoph near Inzlingen (D)

After a couple of hours we came to the farm called Maienbühl. This marks the beginning of the "Eiserne Hand", a part of Switzerland that penetrates for a distance of more than 2 km into Germany like a finger or a spear, all in a forest, with often muddy paths. It took us 45 minutes to cover this "promontory", finally arriving at a place only 200 m behind the same farm!

At the customs of Riehen-Lörrach we were joined by Natalie, her husband Andrew and 2 of their 3 children, Léo, 12 years old and Tessa, 7 years old at the time (the other girl was sick) who were going to do the last kilometres with us. So there were seven of us climbing into the vineyards of Schlipf. This was not so easy because of the steep slope and many houses and private roads. But we were soon down again hiking along a river called Wiese, later passing under the railway and the motorway near the customs post at Otterbach and finally to the customs post Hiltalingerstrasse and the commercial port, where I began my journey on June 5th, 2015. We were greeted by Sally, Elke (Christoph's wife), Inès (Natalie's elder daughter) and my brother Walter who had come specially from Vienna for the occasion.

The main road with the customs post was not the place to celebrate the end of my circuit; we had already invited friends and acquaintances to be on site at the Dreiländereck, more conducive to celebrations, at 3 p.m. Everyone in Kleinhüningen drove there. All I had to do was get into the kayak, wait for everything to be ready on the other side of the water and then paddle the 200 metres that separated me from the Dreiländereck, where about 30 friends and family members were already waiting. Champagne, etc! Later, most of the participants ended the party at the Schiff Restaurant in Kleinhüningen.

The last 200 metres	Reception committee

Of course, I was very happy that my dream had come true. In my head I relived the highlights of the circuit – good days, tiring days, more or less serious incidents, meeting people, and always in the background the encouragement and support of many friends and "fans" who had followed my blogs. I was especially grateful to Sally, who never doubted me, even though she was often concerned about my safety. I was often asked what was THE highlight of the whole circuit. Well, there were many of them, but if I had to pick out one, it must be surely be the Matterhorn!

Information systems

Website

It seemed to me useful for people to be aware of the project and to be able to follow my progress by reading blogs and seeing some pictures. My website www.swiss-perimeter.ch was established by a group working under the name Catalyste.ch. The sections include general information on the project and the Swiss border, a section on other complete or partial circuits that I learned about via the internet, daily blogs and a section "Frontier stories", originally proposed by a good friend and former colleague, which is the basis of a later chapter in this book. There are also pictures of all the mountain guides, all those who accompanied me on various sections of the circuit, all those who helped me as regards the logistics, and an invitation to donate to the charity Medair and a contact form.

Mobile phones, communication

I planned to do a blog every day. This was possible from a mobile phone (iPhone), but only if there was Wi-Fi or a mobile network signal. This was normally the case except in some mountain huts. I tried to publish blogs in three languages, which was a little ambitious, certainly, but appreciated by my "followers" in England especially. With the mobile phone, I could only do them in one language; later, when I could access my PC, I could add pictures and the other languages, if I had time.

To have a contact with Sally, we used the "Locate my iPhone" function, which allowed us to see where the other one was. A condition for this is that both phones were switched on and there was a mobile network signal in the places where we both were. But in these cases we could also just call each other! Phone network signals were often lacking in deep valleys, in border areas, and especially in the mountains, which gave some problems.

Geolocation

I also wanted to have a system of geolocation, with which I could, via my mobile phone, insert a point in a map of Switzerland on my website. I tried to do this 2-3 times a day or every 20 kilometres or so. This worked well via the OwnTracks app – on the condition again that there was a mobile network signal – and it was often the first indication that my "followers" had about my progress well before the daily blog was published. In practice, in the case of a location without a mobile network signal that I wanted to include on the map (e.g. the summit of the Matterhorn), I could communicate the coordinates to Catalyste.ch who would then insert the point manually. The following picture shows what it looked like at the end of 2015.

Preparation and logistics

Planning

As is mentioned in the main text, my elder daughter Sonia suggested I contact the Frost Guiding office in Evolène for hiring mountain guides. She had already done two weeks of ski treks with the director, Graham Frost. He had been living in Valais for a few years with his wife Janine. During a preliminary discussion they declared themselves interested in my project and ready to recruit guides for about five weeks, which would cover the Valais part of the circuit, starting with the Dents Blanches, then part of the Mont Blanc range and the main chain of the Valais Alps from the Grand St-Bernard pass to the Griespass on the borders of Ticino. They found five very qualified and competent guides, all from England or Scotland. This saved me having to recruit guides myself separately for each section.

Graham thought it would be wise to start the section in the Mont Blanc range late June or at the very beginning of July, in order to have the best snow conditions. Working backwards, this fixed my departure in Basel at the beginning of June. I reckoned I could do the western border and Lake Geneva, from Basel to St-Gingolph or a little further in 15 days, in any weather (and in fact I spent 2½ weeks up to the start of the Dent Blanches, above Champéry. For the sections after the Valais, I did not set any precise timing; I would plan mainly on a day-to-day basis.

Hiking and mountain equipment, bicycle

I already had all the equipment I needed except mountain boots adapted to crampons. I bought these at Yosemite in Lausanne, La Sportiva brand. They served me well from St-Gingolph for more than 2 months of intensive use. Unfortunately, I chose a half-size too small – I had to wear very thin socks, which sometimes gave me cold feet in the highest mountains. Furthermore, they showed signs of wear around the sole. A friend, Yves Stettler from Montagne-Show in Le Châble, gave me the correct size in late August. My son Roger lent me a good anorak that was very useful to me and a descendeur (which I finally only used once). He also lent me a mountain bike.

Kayaks

For the kayak sections, I needed two boats, a single and a two-seater. My first grandchild, Natan, had announced from the very beginning that he wanted to do Lake Geneva with me, an offer accepted with pleasure! In a two-seater kayak the 57 km would only take about 9 hours, but alone in a single-seater I would have spent at least 12 hours, not counting headwinds! It was hardly possible to rent the two kayaks needed for the whole season, so I spoke to Passion Nautique in Morges. After discussion, I ordered two at the beginning of May: a "classic" single-seat kayak, "Solo", RTM brand of the Rotomod manufacturer in France, weight 20 kg, and a two-seater, "Biwok Evo Hi-luxe", brand DAG also from the manufacturer Rotomod, weight 34 kg. They had to come from France, but delivery times were not respected. So I had to start with a single-seater kayak loaned by Passion Nautical to help me out and I did not have time to train on it.

Navigation, orientation

My main tool was a Garmin GPS with Swiss topographic maps on a small SIM card in it. This device was very useful to me, even essential, showing me my precise location. It was less useful for planning a route because the screen is very small. Another disadvantage was that the batteries lasted only about 12 to 15 hours – so they were quite run down or even flat after a long day and they usually had to be replaced quite early the next day. I quickly took rechargeable batteries, but it was often difficult or impossible to recharge them in mountain huts. For the "normal" hikes, I prepared extracts of the Swiss topographic maps from map.geo.admin.ch , at a scale of 1: 20,000. I also used the Garmin for daily statistics, that is for walking times, resting times, distances covered and vertical distances climbed or descended.

Physical training

In the end I did not do very much. I do a little gym (for seniors!) once a week during school periods. I did some small hikes in the Vaud Alps, never more than 3-4 hours of walking, but with substantial climbs and descents, but otherwise I relied on the first stages on the western border and in the Jura to reach a suitable degree of fitness. I did not do anything special for the 4000-metre peaks, thinking that I had already done enough of these during my life. As already mentioned, I did not have time to train on the kayak, or to do a lot of cycling. Once the journey started, I did not have any problems as regards fitness.

Logistics and accommodation

Apart from organising and preparing the material and equipment used, including maps and guide-books, the logistics mainly involved transport, so as to have everything available in the right place at the right time. It also included finding places to stay in the valleys. Both Sally and Nona Rowat did this admirably. Sally in the end went around almost the whole border, but on the roads and by car, often with the kayak and the bicycle.

For the first two weeks I booked every night in advance in B&Bs, dormitories or small hotels near my arrival points. But having lost half a day early on (because of a stomach problem), their locations were no longer optimal. We changed or cancelled where it was possible, and if not, we had to accept some extra kilometres in the car! Subsequently I always tried to phone the day before or even in the morning, or we looked for something on arrival. In the mountains we used mountain huts, agritourism sites or bivouac shelters. I thought initially of bivouacking to avoid going down to remote huts, but in practice it was better to go down as much as 1000 metres or more to a hut to avoid carrying bivouac equipment. In the end I only bivouacked once during the whole circuit (with Peter at the beginning of the Grisons frontier).

Frontier stories

All along the frontier there are places that are interesting for historical or geographical reasons, or because the boundary follows an unusual path. A series of "frontier stories" was originally proposed for my website by a good friend and a former colleague, François Chastellain, to whom I am very grateful. These "stories" deal with various topics, historical or geographical, often anecdotes, for various points of the border, interesting information that is not easily found in guides or tourist brochures. I edited a few of these stories, translated almost all of them from French into English and German, and added some myself when I passed interesting places or learned interesting things. Many of these stories are incorporated into the main text of this book but without the references. In this section you will find either the complete text or supplementary information and all the references. Many references are only in French or German.

Tripoints – Dreiländereck in Basel, et al

The Dreiländereck represents the frontier point common to the three countries: Switzerland, France and Germany (although the real tripoint lies 150 m away in the middle of the river).

The five other tripoints are less well known and for some of them less accessible:

> The Mont Dolent. The frontier between Switzerland, Italy and France is not at the summit but 71 m lower down where the north and west ridges meet.
>
> In the Lower Engadine, on the north slope of Piz Lad, 628 m below the summit (Switzerland / Italy / Austria).
>
> Two tripoints between Austria, Switzerland and Liechtenstein, one on the Naafkopf, the other in the middle of the bed of the Rhine.
>
> The last one, between Austria, Germany and Switzerland, is in the middle of Lake Constance, but there is no international treaty which fixes it.

References: https://en.wikipedia.org/wiki/Dreiländereck_(Basel) and https://fr.wikipedia.org/wiki/Liste_des_tripoints_de_Suisse (in French).

Bänggenspitz or Benkenspitz

See also pages 8/9 of the main text.

The municipal boundary in the forest northwest of Biel-Benken forms a wedge between the French municipalities Neuwiller and Leymen. I suspect this strip of land was formerly an aristocratic hunting reserve. Biel-Benken was sold in 1526 by the Schaler knights (Schalberg Castle, Pfeffingen) to the city of Basel. This strange border geometry in Benkenspitz was documented in 1620 by means of a map drawn by the Basel painter Hans Bock the Elder (1550-1624), commissioned by the Basel government. The frontier was surveyed in 1746 and the markers completed. The Basel bishop's staff symbol was added to the boundary stones on the Biel-Benken side. Another survey was carried out 1816.

The "entrance" to Benkenspitz - "Between the Holzmatten" - is about 62 metres wide, and is the narrowest part of Switzerland! (69 metres between boundary stones 126 and 109.)

Reference:
https://www.geocaching.com/seek/cache_details.aspx?wp=GC3HGNJ&title=im-banggenspitz-spitz (in German)
Photo of 1620 map:
http://www.regionatur.ch/Themen/Personen/Kartografen?a=image&bild_id=10744

The largest beech tree in north-western Switzerland

See also page 11 of the main text.

The tree stands at about 455 metres of altitude in the middle of a forest, between the boundary stones 61 and 62. The long branchless trunk is also very unusual in that it divides into three equal forks only at the height of 17 metres.

Reference: https://www.so.ch/fileadmin/internet/vwd/vwd-awjf-wald/pdf/Waldwanderungen/Mariastein/WWSo_Nr_5_Postentafeln_46-55.pdf
(go to notice board no. 47) (in German).

"Borne des Trois Puissances" (Frontier stone of the three powers)

See page 12 of the main text.

The "Borne des Trois Puissances" is an old frontier stone that marks the tripoint where, from 1871 to 1918, France, Germany and Switzerland met. It is the highest of the 3 stones present in this place. It was placed on September 28, 1871 (the current version was installed in 1890) following the peace treaty ending the Franco-Prussian War of 1870-1871 which ceded Alsace and Lorraine to the German Empire.

There are two other stones at this location. One, marked "F" and "D" and the number 4056, is the last marker of a series that was set up to define the new border between France and Germany from Luxembourg to Switzerland. The other, smaller and more degraded, is in fact only the base of a frontier stone dating from the Habsburg era when Alsace was part of the Holy Roman Empire until the Peace of Westphalia in 1648.

During the years that followed 1871, this place became a real place of patriotic pilgrimage for the French.

Reference: https://fr.wikipedia.org/wiki/Borne_des_Trois_Puissances and https://www.beurnevesin.ch/index.php/tourisme/borne-des-trois-puissances (both in French).

The right bank of the Doubs

See page 13 of the main text.

Reference: http://www.eau21.ch/etude_33.html (in French).

The slippage of the Vraconnaz peat bog

Not mentioned in the main text.

Below the first frontier marker Vaud / France coming from the canton of Neuchâtel, near the Col des Etroits, is the magnificent peat bog, or "Mouille", of Vraconnaz (pronounced: Vraconne) which slopes downhill slightly.

Over 30 years ago, during the night of September 26th, 1987, the upper layer made of peat broke off and slipped for 300 metres towards the Sécha hill. From a smooth landscape covered with sphagnum moss and bog bilberry, the bog became a collection of shapeless heaps. Time has done its work since then and the signs of the slippage are no longer as spectacular as in 1987. Worthy of protection, the peat bog became the first nature reserve in Switzerland in 1911. It is now owned by Pro Natura, and enjoys protection since the 1990s by virtue of its status as a raised bog and a marshy site of national importance.

Reference:
https://www.bafu.admin.ch/bafu/fr/home/themes/biodiversite/dossiers/premiere-reserve-naturelle-pro-natura.html (in French).

The boundary stones on the border between Vaud and France

There are no less than 309 boundary stones, not including intermediate markers between the Swiss Canton of Vaud and France. Some of them date back to the sixteenth century, well before the surveyors!

Jean-François Robert, forest engineer and former head of the Vaud cantonal forestry department did useful work by drawing up an inventory of these boundary stones (see reference below). In this brochure, illustrated by the author, we learn almost everything about the dates and symbols carved on the ancient stones. We also learn that when the boundary stone was put in place, a volume equivalent to 1 dm^3 of charcoal was placed underneath it as well as two "witnesses" made by breaking a brick in half, which could be authenticated by fitting the two halves together. Why? Mystery!

References (both in French):
Vieilles bornes en pays de Vaud, J.-F. Robert, édition "L'industriel sur bois", 1980, 30 pages (the brochure is available at the museum of the Aubonne Arboretum).

Histoire de bornes, O. Cavaleri, éditions Slatkine, 2011-2014 (4 books on the boundary stones between France and Switzerland.

The "rectangle" of Bois d'Amont

See also pages 19/20 of the main text.

As part of the revision of the Franco-Swiss border in 1863 (Treaty of the Dappes Valley of 1862, see the following item), Switzerland received some 703 hectares of territory on the western slope of the Noirmont between La Cure and Bois d'Amont.

As a result, a number of dairies and cheese factories would have no longer been in France but in Switzerland, thus cutting off the inhabitants of Les Rousses and

Bois d'Amont from their traditional sources of dairy products, for which residents would then have to pay customs duties.

A Bois d'Amont resident, Olivier Arbel, made a proposal to maintain some cheese factories in France and encouraged the local authorities to send a petition to Paris. This petition was only partially successful, in order to respect the equivalence of the surfaces exchanged, but two cheese factories finally remained French, which explains this surprising shape of the line of the frontier.

Explanations given in http://www.dodtour.com/index2.php , Logbook, 22 September 2011, in French.

The Treaty of the Dappes Valley

See page 19 of the main text.

There have not been many corrections to the Swiss border since the Congress of Vienna in 1815. The Treaty of the Dappes Valley is a notable exception. Signed in December 1862, this treaty ended a long-standing French claim. After much discussion and exchange of territory, the treaty signed between the Swiss Federal Council, and "His Majesty the Emperor of the French" precisely defines the exchange of territory (about 700 hectares).

Article 3 of the Treaty states: "The original inhabitants of that part of the Dappes Valley being returned to France under this Treaty remain French, unless they declare, within a year, to opt for Swiss citizenship, in which case they may maintain their home and business in the Empire's territory". An equivalent paragraph deals with the fate of those French who found themselves in Switzerland.

Reference: https://www.admin.ch/opc/fr/classified-compilation/18620007/186302200000/0.132.349.24.pdf (in French).

The fire in St-Gingolph

See page 26 of the main text.

Reference:
http://www.livresdeguerre.net/forum/contribution.php?index=39320&surl=UF
and
http://www.st-gingolph.com/tragedie/ (both in French).

Cervin or Servin ?

In his book "The mountain and its names" Jules Guex, well-known toponymist and eminent patois speaker, devoted a whole chapter to the French name of the Matterhorn, a subject of heated debate among linguists of the past century.

The author first comments that whereas well used cols or passes were given names in the Middle Ages, this was not the case for the surrounding mountains, which did not interest travellers before the age of mountaineering. The Theodul Pass bore different names in the past including Silvius Mons (mons in Latin may also mean col). The origin of silvius must be sought in silva "where there are forests." Subsequently, the name of the col was attributed to the mountain as Mount Servin until Horace Bénédict de Saussure renames it – perhaps as a result of a spelling error – Mont Cervin.

Jules Guex concludes with these words: "If the Federal Office of Topography wants to respect the historical and linguistic truth as attested by the most ancient documents, they should in the future write Matterhorn / Monte Servino / Mont Servin on our maps". Jules Guex was not heard!

Reference: La montagne et ses noms, Jules Guex, ed. Rouge 1946, 2nd ed. Pillet Martigny 1976 (in French).

The disaster at Gondo

See page 52 of the main text.

In Gondo today, next to the hotel, one can visit a small museum dedicated to the gold mines that the Stockalper family had operated from the 17th century. The few vrenelis that still exist made from Gondo gold have become very valuable (up to CHF 68'000. - !).

Reference: http://www.rts.ch/archives/tv/information/3438595-gondo-sinistre.html (video 8 min, in French).

Directly above the Simplon tunnel

See also page 53 of the main text.

On the main frontier ridge there is a frontier marker at 2815 m, located directly above the Simplon tunnel which crosses under the mountain almost 2100 metres lower down, and 100 metres from an intermediate summit called Tunnelspitz.

The construction of the first tunnel between 1898 and 1905 was heroic - more than 45°C inside the tunnel! – because the drilling machines were still rudimentary. One can see such a drill, as well as the iron gate intended to stop the water from entering the construction site, in the north wing of the Palais de Rumine in Lausanne.

Reference: https://notrehistoire.ch/entries/RL28L6pOYKA (in French).

The Gries Glacier, and what remains of it . . .

See pages 56/57, section on glacier shrinkage.

In the second picture one can make out the wind turbine installed in 2011 by SwissWinds. This pilot project at 2465 m altitude is the highest in Europe.

References:
https://www.swisseduc.ch/glaciers/alps/griesgletscher/griesgletscher-en.html (with better photos) and
http://www.rts.ch/info/suisse/3430066-une-eolienne-a-2465-metres-d-altitude-en-valais.html (in French).

Bosco / Gurin

See page 61 of the main text.

References: https://en.wikipedia.org/wiki/Bosco/Gurin and
http://www.hls-dhs-dss.ch/textes/f/F2257.php (in French).

The baths of Craveggia

See page 64 of the main text.

References http://www.beat-glauser.ch/vocaglia_bilder_8.htm (in German) and
https://www.myswitzerland.com/en-ch/experiences/the-old-thermal-baths-of-craveggia/
Photo in main text from: https://www.gogoterme.com/terme-libere-di-bagni-di-craveggia.html .

The isolation of Indemini

See pages 66/67 of the main text.

Reference: https://www.myswitzerland.com/en-ch/destinations/indemini/ and https://www.ticinotopten.ch/en/villages/indemini .

Boundary stones dated 1559

See pages 68/69 of the main text.

Reference: http://www.hls-dhs-dss.ch/textes/f/F8898.php .(in French)
Better photo: https://www.flickr.com/photos/cochabamba/3474052940/in/photostream/ .

The Monte Generoso railway

Barely mentioned in the main text, pages 71/72, but with two pictures.

Monte Generoso (1700 m) is well known to families in Ticino. The 360° view is exceptional and on clear days one can see from Milan to the Gran Paradiso and from Monte Rosa to the Bernina range. Since 1890, a cog-wheel train takes visitors effortlessly from Capolago to the summit. The line is now electrified but a steam train (with an 1890 locomotive!) provides the service on special occasions. In 1941, the founder of Migros, Gottlieb Duttweiler, bought the rail facilities that were then adrift and transformed Monte Generoso into tourist site of national importance.

Because of construction work on Monte Generoso, rail traffic was temporarily suspended in 2015 and reopened in 2017.

Reference: https://www.montegeneroso.ch/en/monte-generoso/history .

The enclave of Campione d'Italia

Mentioned in the main text, page 73.

Campione d'Italia is first and foremost the Municipal Casino. The striking edifice of Mario Botta built in 2007 has the merit being seen from Lugano, day and night. But it is true that with a surface area of 55'000 m^2 it is difficult to go unnoticed! It declared bankruptcy in July 2018. Since it was the territory's main source of income, the financial future of the enclave is compromised. It is also a tax haven where citizens pay only half the taxes that would be paid by other Italians. The border with Switzerland only exists on maps, because in fact many details are reminiscent of the Ticino: car number plates, health insurance, not forgetting that the Swiss franc is widely used.

Reference: https://en.wikipedia.org/wiki/Campione_d%27Italia .

The Swiss Customs Museum at Cantine di Gandria

See pages 81/82, section on smuggling.

Reference: https://www.ezv.admin.ch/ezv/en/home/the-fca/customs-museum-in-cantine-di-gandria--lugano/das-museum.html .

The formidable Splügen

See pages 76/77 of the main text.

Reference: http://www.hls-dhs-dss.ch/textes/f/F8823.php (in French).

Lei valley and lake

Not mentioned in the main text.

The Lei valley, Italian territory since 1863, was uninhabited and therefore well suited for a hydroelectric facility. The dam built in 1962 required a formal agreement between Italy and Switzerland. Since the lake represented a danger for the Swiss valleys below in the event of a rupture, the Confederation requested to keep the dam under its authority. By way of compensation, some territory downstream from the dam was transferred to Italy.

Such cross-border agreements related to the operation of dams are not uncommon. A good example is the Emosson dam located entirely in Swiss territory but collecting waters from the Mont Blanc massif. The power station is located in France just across the border from Le Châtelard. Another example is Lake Livigno near the Ofenpass.

Incidentally, the Valle di Lei is the only Italian territory whose waters drain into the Rhine and eventually reach the North Sea!

Reference: http://de.wikipedia.org/wiki/Lago_di_Lei (in German).

The Badile of Riccardo Cassin

The Bregaglia range consists of magnificent granite, much younger than those of the Grimsel and of Mont Blanc that were formed before the birth of the Alps. This coarse-grained granite has been a delight for climbers since the 1930s.

In 1937, Riccardo Cassin and his climbing partners were the first to conquer the north-east face of Piz Badile that was a terrifying mountain face at the time. Cassin played a decisive role in the development of materials adapted to the extreme conditions of mountain climbing (such as climbing shoes, for example). He died in his bed at the age of 100 years and 7 months which for a man who took so many risks in his life is a real achievement!

Reference: http://en.wikipedia.org/wiki/Riccardo_Cassin .

Between the Rhine and Old Rhine

See also page 126 of the main text.

Major projects are under way to give the Alpine Rhine upstream from Lake Constance a more pronounced natural character.

References: http://www.hls-dhs-dss.ch/textes/f/F8768.php?topdf=1 (in French) and http://www.alpenrhein.net/ (in German) and https://kids.iksr.org/en/12-14/the-rhine/where-is-the-rhine/alpenrheinbodensee/ which includes an expanded version of the photo on page 129 of the main text.

The Rhine Delta and "boundary stone" seventy-three

See also pages 129/130 of the main text.

At the mouth of the Old Rhine in Lake Constance there was a frontier marker (number 73), shown on the older Swiss national maps up to 2013, in the lake some way from the shore. This was not a physical marker but a point calculated from other markers which are located on either side of the Rhine. The axis of the Rhine is defined from a whole set of such markers.

Reference: https://en.wikipedia.org/wiki/Rhine_delta_(Lake_Constance) and http://www.rheindelta.com/start.html (in German).

The uncertain crossings of MF Romanshorn

See page 130 of the main text.

References: http://fr.wikipedia.org/wiki/Navigation_sur_le_lac_de_Constance (in French) and http://www.welt.de/print-welt/article661125/Bodensee-ist-voelkerrechtlich-Niemandsland.html (in German).

Reichenau Abbey and Arenenberg castle

See page 131 of the main text.

References: http://fr.wikipedia.org/wiki/Abbaye_de_Reichenau (in French) and https://napoleonmuseum.tg.ch/en.html/7107 .

The bombing of Schaffhausen

See page 135 of the main text.

References: http://www.schaffhausen-nostalgie-foto.ch/266,0,schaffhausen-bombardiert-,index,0.html (in German, includes photo in main text) and https://www.swissinfo.ch/eng/-swisshistorypics_when-the-americans-bombed-a-swiss-city/44865520 and https://en.wikipedia.org/wiki/Bombings_of_Switzerland_in_World_War_II .

The Rhine Falls

See also pages 136/137 of the main text.

Fifty km below the falls, the river Aare, the main tributary of the Rhine in Switzerland, brings much more water than the Rhine itself. The Rhine has different flow rates between summer and winter (in Basel: 1500 m^3/s in June compared with 700 m^3/s in January). But exceptional years are not uncommon: in 1858 the flow in Basel was only 202 m^3/s, about 50 m^3 more than the Rhone in Geneva. Difficult to navigate under these conditions!

Reference: https://en.wikipedia.org/wiki/Rhine_Falls .

Laufenburg

See pages 140/141 of the main text.

References: http://histoire-suisse.geschichte-schweiz.ch/republique-helvetique-1798.html and
http://www.hls-dhs-dss.ch/textes/f/F1742.php (both in French).

The bridge of Augusta Raurica

See pages 142/143 of the main text.

References: http://www.augustaraurica.ch/en/ and especially
https://www.augustaraurica.ch/en/visit/sights/bridgehead/ .

Daily log 1 - itinerary

Total →	2480	757:25	
Aver. →	22	~6:30	
Date	Day	km	hh:mm	Itinerary
2015				
05.06	001	29.7	06:50	Kleinhüningen - Allschwil - Schönenbuch - Benken - Bättwil - Flüh
06.06	002	40.0	09:00	Flüh - Rodersdorf - Burg im Leimental - Rämelsberg - Klösterli - Lucelle - customs post Miécourt
07.06	003	7.4	02:10	Customs post Miécourt - forest near Bonfol
08.06	004	33.8	07:30	Forest near Bonfol - Beurnevésin - customs post Boncourt - Les Bornes, near Bure
09.06	005	43.1	10:30	Les Bornes - Fahy - Damvant - customs post Réclère (caves) - Montancy - Brémoncourt
10.06	006	39.0	08:30	Brémoncourt - Epiquerez - Clairbief - Goumois - Biaufond
11.06	007	33.4	06:10	Biaufond - Châtelot power plant - Lac des Brenets - Le Col-des-Roches
12.06	008	30.7	07:20	Le Col-des-Roches - L'Ecrenaz - La Petite Ronde, north of Verrières
13.06	009	32.3	09:30	La Petite Ronde - customs post Les Verrières - tripoint F-NE-VD - Col de l'Aiguillon - frontier stone 43, north of Ballaigues
14.06	010	10.2	04:30	Frontier stone 43 - customs post Vallorbe - Cabane du Mont d'Or - La Petite Echelle
15.06	011	32.0	08:15	La Petite Echelle - Refuge du Poteau - Roche Champion - Chalet Gaillard, north of Bois d'Amont
16.06	012	37.5	09:10	Chalet Gaillard - Bois d'Amont - La Cure - La Baudichonne - La Rippe
17.06	013	33.4	07:00	La Rippe - Crassier - customs post Chavannes-de-Bogis - Collex-Bossy - Ferney-Voltaire - customs post Meyrin
18.06	014	48.6	07:30	Customs post Meyrin - La Plaine - Chancy - Bois de Chancy - Sézegnin - Soral - customs post Perly

164

Date	No.	km	Time	Route
19.06	015	48.9	04:20	Customs post Perly - Veyrier - Thônex - Juvigny - Monniaz - Gy - Hermance
20.06	016	49.0	07:55	Hermance - St-Gingolph
21.06				
22.06	017	23.8	08:50	St-Gingolph - Les Cornettes de Bise - Col de Recon
23.06	018	29.2	07:45	Col de Recon - Tour de Don - Pas de Morgins - Portes de l'Hiver - Le Lapisa
24.06	019	19.0	10:30	Le Lapisa - Col de Bossetan - Pas au Taureau - Dent de Barme - Refuge de la Vogealle CAF
25.06	020	17.0	11:00	Refuge de la Vogealle - Mont Ruan - Col de Tanneverge - bivouac hut Vallon de Tenneverge
26.06	021	16.0	09:45	Bivouac hut - Col de Tanneverge - Lac du Vieux Emosson - Le Cheval Blanc - Emosson dam
27.06				
28.06	022	16.5	04:50	Emosson dam - customs post Le Châtelard - Aiguillette - Col de Balme
29.06	023	10.9	06:00	Col de Balme - Pointe des Grands - Aiguilles du Tour - Cabane du Trient CAS
30.06	024	12.9	06:50	Cabane du Trient - Fenêtre de Saleinaz - Col du Chardonnet - Aiguille d'Argentière - Refuge d'Argentière CAF
01.07	025	14.1	06:30	Refuge d'Argentière - Col du Tour Noir - La Croix de Lognan
02.07	026	6.9	03:10	La Peule (Val Ferret) - Grand Col Ferret - bivouac hut Fiorio CAAI
03.07	027	12.9	08:40	Bivouac hut - Mont Dolent - Grand Col Ferret - La Peule
04.07	028	17.8	08:10	Gd St-Bernard road at 2100 m - Col de St-Rhémy - Col des Angroniettes - Mt Fourchon - Col du Gd St-Bernard
05.07	029	13.7	10:00	Bourg St-Bernard - Col d'Annibal - Mont Vélan - Cabane du Vélan CAS
06.07	030	5.0	01:40	Cabane du Vélan - above Bourg-St-Pierre at 1790 m - (Cabane de Chanrion CAS, by car)
07.07	031	11.5	06:00	Cabane de Chanrion - Bivouac de l'Aiguillette à la Singla CAS - Col d'Otemma - Bivouac de l'Aiguillette
08.07	032	17.0	08:30	Bivouac de l'Aiguillette - Col de l'Evêque - Plan Bertol - Cabane de Bertol CAS
09.07	033	18.9	08:30	Cabane de Bertol - Tête Blanche - Stockji - Zmuttgletscher - Chalbermatta - Zmutt - Zermatt
10.07	034	7.8	02:10	Klein Matterhorn - Testa Grigia - (Plan Maison, by cable car) - Rifugio Duca degli Abruzzi all'Oriondé

11.07	035	13.1	14:00	Rifugio Oriondé - Matterhorn - Rifugio Oriondé
12.07	036	11.5	04:00	Rifugio Oriondé - Plan Maison - (Testa Grigia, by cable car) - Klein Matterhorn - Breithorn - Klein Matterhorn
13.07	037	9.9	07:00	Klein Matterhorn - Pollux - Castor - Rifugio Quintino Sella CAI
14.07	038	10.8	07:20	Rifugio Quintino Sella - Ludwigshöhe - Parrotspitze - Signalkuppe (Capanna Regina Margherita CAI)
15.07	039	10.4	07:10	Capanna Margherita - Zumsteinspitze - Dufourspitze - Nordend - Monte-Rosa-Hütte SAC
16.07	040	18.2	10:30	Monte-Rosa-Hütte - Cima di Jazzi - Stockhorn - Gornergrat
17.07				
18.07	041	7.9	02:55	Mattmark dam - Rifugio Oberto-Maroli (CAI)
19.07	042	9.0	12:00	Rifugio Oberto-Maroli - Joderhorn - Spechhorn - Jazzihorn - Vorder Latelhorn - Bivacco Camposecco CAI
20.07	043	24.5	08:30	Bivacco Camposecco - Passo delle Coronette - Rifugio Andolla CAI - Passo d'Andolla - Gondo
21.07	044	22.4	10:20	Simplon hospice - Breithornpass - Monte Leone - Breithornpass - Monte-Leone-Hütte SAC
22.07	045	14.6	05:15	Monte-Leone-Hütte - Wasenhorn - Monte-Leone-Hütte - Chaltwasserpass - Rifugio Città di Arona CAI (Alpe Veglia)
23.07	046	27.5	08:15	Rifugio Arona - Passo di Valtendra - Scatta d'Orogna - Alpe Dèvero - Crampiolo - Albrunpass - Binntalhütte SAC
24.07	047	25.0	14:00	Binntalhütte - Ofenhorn - Hohsandhorn - Blinnenhorn - Griespass - Capanna Corno-Gries CAS
25.07	048	2.3		Capanna Corno-Gries - Cruina (postbus stop)
26.07	049	2.3	00:40	Cruina (postbus stop) - Capanna Corno-Gries CAS
27.07	050	19.7	10:20	Capanna Corno-Gries - Passo San Giacomo - Bocchetta di Val Maggia - Basòdino - Rifugio Piano delle Creste
28.07	051	13.0	07:30	Rifugio Piano delle Creste - Bocchetta della Cròsa - Pizzo Cazzòla - Capanna Grossalp (Bosco / Gurin)
29.07	052	9.4	03:00	Capanna Grossalp - Passo Quadrella - Cimalmotto
30.07	053	21.2	08:15	Cimalmotto - Passo della Cavegna - Capanna Alpe Arena - Passo del Busan - Pilone - Capanna Alpe Salèi
31.07	054	18.6	07:00	Capanna Alpe Salèi - Comologno - Alpe Lombardone - Pescia Lunga - Lionza - Borgnone
01.08				

02.08	055	20.0	09:20	Pian del Barch - Testa di Misello - Rocce del Gridone - Gridone - Cortaccio - customs post Valmara
03.08	056	14.8	04:30	Customs post Valmara - customs post Dirinella - Covreto - Paión - Alpe Cedullo
04.08	057	27.5	07:40	Alpe Cedullo - Indemini - Pòla - Monte Lema - Cavagnino - Sessa
05.08	058	17.8	03:30	Customs post Cavagno (Suino) - Termine - Ponte Tresa - customs post Brusino-Basso Ceresio
06.08	059	35.4	09:00	Terniciolo - Serpiano - Poncione d'Arzo - Arzo - San Pietro - customs post Stabio - Novazzano - Pedrinate - Chiasso
07.08	060	28.5	07:30	Chiasso - Sagno - Monte Bisbino - Poncione di Cabbio - Passo Bonello - pt 727 on the road north of Muggio
08.08	061	29.8	06:50	Pt 727 - Monte Generoso - Cima dei Torrioni - Lanzo d'Intelvi - Santa Margherita - Oria
09.08	062	3.6	01:00	Gandria - Brè
10.08	063	41.9	11:00	Brè - Capanna Pairolo - Passo di San Lucio - Gazzirola - Bocchetta di Sommafiume - Passo San Jorio - Capanna Gesero
11.08	064	14.2	06:30	Capanna Gesero - Cima di Cugn - Bocchetta di Camedo - bivouac at 2200 m, below Cardinello
12.08	065	16.2	08:10	Bivouac - Passo del Orso - Bocchetta di Correggia - Bocchetta del Notar - Capanna Righetti-Fibbioli (Alp del Lago)
13.08	066	14.2	06:00	Alp del Lago - Cama - (postbus and car) - Splügenpass - Pizzo Tambo - Splügenpass
14.08	067	22.0	06:40	Splügenpass - Rifugio Bertacchi CAI - Pass da Niemet - pt 2843 - Valle di Sterla - Madesimo
15.08				Madesimo - Chiavenna - Castasegna (postbuses)
16.08	068	18.8	08:00	Bondo - Bocchetta della Tegiola - Bivacco Pedroni del Prà CAI - Passo Porcellizzo - Rifugio Gianetti CAI
17.08	069	3.2	01:30	Rifugio Gianetti - ca. 2810 m below Pizzo Badile - Rifugio Gianetti
18.08	070	5.2	03:00	Rifugio Gianetti - ca. 2660 m below Passo del Camerozzo - Rifugio Gianetti - (Sondalo hospital, by helicopter)
30.08	071	22.1	08:30	Campascio - Viano - Tegial - frontier stone 13 (pt 2647 m) - Pass Portun - Grüm Sur - Viano
31.08	072	20.2	10:15	Cable car Albigna - Capanna da l'Albigna CAS - Cima di Castello - Vadret del Forno - Capanna del Forno (CAS)
01.09	073	14.4	05:50	Capanna del Forno - Sella del Forno - Monte del Forno - Passo del Muretto - Alp da Cavloc - Passo del Maloja

02.09			
03.09	074	23.6	06:20	Brusio - Cavaione - Pescia Bassa - Col d'Anzana - Lughina - Campocologno
04.09	075	14.4	05:15	Motta (above Poschiavo) - Braga - Bocchetta di Braga - L'Om - Pass da l'Om - Albertüsc - Motta
05.09	076	9.2	03:30	Somdoss - Plan dal Fopal - Pass da Canfinal - La Casina - Somdoss
06.09				Diavolezza (by cable car)
07.09				(return by cable car)
01.10	077	6.0	01:30	La Rösa (Val Poschiavo) - Rifugio Saoseo CAS
02.10	078	16.4	06:30	Rifugio Saoseo - Pass da Sach - Lagh da Val Viola - frontier stone 11, Pass da Val Viola - Rifugio Saoseo
03.10	079	18.7	07:30	Rifugio Saoseo - Pass da Val Mera - Piz Ursera - Forcola di Livigno - La Rösa
04.10	080	3.6	01:20	Baitel del Gras degli Agnelli (on the road to Forcola di Livigno) - La Stretta (col) - Baitel del Gras degli Agnelli
11.10	081	24.3	08:00	Alpe Campaccio (on road to Livigno) - Piz la Stretta - Monte Garone - Fuorcla Federia - Valle di Federia, at 2010 m
12.10	082	22.2	04:10	Punt dal Gall (Lago di Livigno) - path below Alpe del Gallo - Passo di Fraéle - La Bocchetta (Lago di Cancano dam)
13.10	083	17.5	04:40	La Bocchetta (Lago di Cancano dam) - Bocchetta di Forcola - Pass Umbrail - Stilfserjoch/Giogo dello Stelvio
22.10	084	14.2	10:45	Stilfserjoch - 5 summits on the border to the north - Alp Prasüra - Gasthaus Alpenrose on the road to Pass Umbrail
23.10	085	15.1	06:15	Road to Pass Umbrail, at 1870 m - shepherds hut Pin Grond, pt 2378 - Val Pisch - Müstair village
24.10	086	15.0	06:55	Pt 1499 m above Müstair - Plaun Radond - Piz Chavalatsch - Rifairscharte - Puntweil - customs post Müstair
02.11	087	19.3	08:30	Müstair - Piz Terza / Urtirolaspitz - Fuorcla Starlex - Val d'Avigna at 1530 m
03.11	088	25.4	07:40	Pt. 1829 m above Schlinig - Sesvennahütte - Schlinigpass - Rasasserscharte - Rojental - Reschen (Resia)

04.11	089	12.6	04:40	Reschner Alm - Grubenjoch - Piz Lad - tripoint Switzerland-Italy-Austria - Reschner Alm
05.11	090	19.0	01:55	Customs post Martina (Martinsbruck) - border at Schalkl (A) - Vinadi - Acla da Fans - customs post Spissermühle
06.11	091	18.9	06:10	Alp Trida Skihaus - Alp Bella - Grübelekopf - Flimjoch - Alptrider Sattel - road to Samnaun, at 1748 m, near Plan
07.11	092	27.9	07:40	Samnaun village - Zeblasjoch - Fuorcla Val Gronda - Fimberpass - Griosch - pt 1506 on the road above Sent
2016				
20.06	093	84.3	07:35	FL-CH border on the Rhine near Sargans - customs post Diepoldsau - Alter Rhein - Rheinspitz - Romanshorn
21.06	094	48.6	05:25	Romanshorn - Kreuzlingen - Konstanz - Ermatingen landing stage - Eschenz-Unterdorf
22.06	095	34.1	07:30	Customs post Stein am Rhein/Öhningen (D) - customs post Ramsen - Spiesshof - Rauhenberg - Rhine bridge at Diessenhofen
23.06	096	73.1	06:45	Diessenhofen - Thayngen - Egghof - Schwarze Staa - Hoher Randen - Schleitheim - customs post Oberwiesen
24.06	097	51.3	04:30	Customs post Oberwiesen - customs post Trasadingen - customs post Altenberg/Nohl (on the Rhine); circuit of the enclave of Büsingen
28.06	098	8.2	01:55	Galtür - Jamtalhütte
29.06	099	13.5	04:50	Jamtalhütte - Kronenjoch - Grenzeckkopf - Pass Futschöl - Jamtalhütte
30.06	100	7.9	02:05	Jamtalhütte - Galtür; Guarda - Chamonna Tuoi CAS
01.07	101	9.4	04:45	Chamonna Tuoi - Fuorcla Vermunt - Dreiländerspitz - Wiesbadener Hütte
02.07	102	13.5	05:40	Wiesbadener Hütte - Piz Buin - Fuorcla dal Cunfin - Silvrettapass - Silvrettahütte SAC
03.07	103	12.2	08:40	Silvrettahütte - Signalhorn - Egghorn - Silvrettahorn - Rotflue - Rote Furka - Silvrettahütte
04.07	104	16.7	07:05	Silvrettahütte - Scharte - Plattenjoch - Seetalhütte SAC - Sardasca (above Klosters)
05.07				
06.07	105	22.3	06:55	Schlappin - Carnäirajoch - Hinterberg - Valzifenzer Joch - Schlappiner Joch - Schlappin

07.07	106	24.9	07:55	Schlappin - Rätschenjoch - Gafier Joch - upper cable car station Gargellen - Schlappiner Joch - Schlappin
08.07	107	24.4	07:35	Cable car Gargellen - Gafier Joch - Riedchopf - Plasseggenpass - Tilisunahütte ÖAV - Sulzfluh - Carschinahütte SAC
09.07	108	27.0	06:45	Carschinahütte - Schweizertor - Verajöchli - Douglasshütte ÖAV - Lüner Krinne - bus stop Leidl (near Vandans)
10.07	109	14.3	05:10	Douglasshütte (Lünersee) - Totalphütte ÖAV - Schesaplana - Gamsluggen - Schesaplanahütte
11.07	110	14.0	04:50	Schesaplanahütte - Gross Furgga - Barthümeljoch - Pfälzerhütte LAV - Naafkopf - Pfälzerhütte
12.07	111	17.5	04:30	Pfälzerhütte - Sücka - Triesenberg - Triesen
27.07	112	45.3	05:00	Nohl footbridge - Rheinau - Ellikon am Rhein (German side) - Rafzerfeld border - Eglisau (Rheinsfelden) power plant
03.08	113	41.9	05:00	Eglisau (Rheinsfelden) power plant - Bad Zurzach - Koblenz - Leibstadt - Laufenburg
04.08	114	44.2	03:50	Laufenburg - Stein AG - Wallbach - Rheinfelden power plant - Kaiseraugst - customs post Riehen-Grenzacherstrasse
06.08	115	27.4	06:10	Customs post Riehen-Grenzacherstrasse - "Eiserne Hand" - customs post Riehen - customs post Hiltalingerstrasse - Dreiländerspitz

170

The records

Vertical distance up in one day

10.08.2015	2740 m
16.08.2015	2620 m
22.06.2015	2610 m

Vertical distance down in one day

02.08.2015	2390 m
20.07.2015	2300 m
31.07.2015	2250 m

Total vertical distance ↑↓ in one day

Daily log 2 effort

Total →	2480	1866	422	192	121530	125920	-4390	757:50
Aver. →	22				1066	1105		~ 6:30
Date	km	Foot	Bike	Kayak	↑ m	↓ m	diff m	hh:mm
2015								
05.06	29.7	21.7	5.0	3.0	930	800	130	06:50
06.06	40.0	29.0	11.0	0.0	1 275	1 165	110	09:00
07.06	7.4	7.4	0.0	0.0	115	135	-20	02:10
08.06	33.8	29.8	4.0	0.0	820	730	90	07:30
09.06	43.1	43.1	0.0	0.0	1 420	1 560	-140	10:30
10.06	39.0	27.0	12.0	0.0	1 080	890	190	08:30
11.06	33.4	27.4	0.0	6.0	810	500	310	06:10
12.06	30.7	30.7	0.0	0.0	1 160	950	210	07:20
13.06	32.3	32.2	0.0	0.0	1 390	1 270	120	09:30
14.06	10.2	10.2	0.0	0.0	780	900	-120	04:30
15.06	32.0	32.0	0.0	0.0	750	680	70	08:15
16.06	37.5	37.5	0.0	0.0	950	1 600	-650	09:10
17.06	33.4	26.4	0.0	7.0	90	190	-100	07:00
18.06	48.6	8.4	37.1	3.1	180	170	10	07:30

10.08.2015	2740 + 1780 = 4520 m							
24.06.2015	2200 + 2090 = 4290 m							
24.07.2015	2160 + 2090 = 4250 m							
Hours on the move in one day								
11.07.2015	13h30 (+ 1/2h stops)							
24.07.2015	13h30 (+ 1/2h stops)							
19.07.2015	12h (+ 1h stops)							
Distance in one day								
On foot								
09.06.2015	43.1 km							
10.08.2105	41.9 km							
By bicycle								
23.06.2016	73.1 km							
20.06.2016	56.5 km							
By kayak								

19.06	015	48.9	0.0	48.9	0.0	280	360	-80	04:20
20.06	016	49.0	0.0	0.0	49.0	0	0	0	07:55
21.06									
22.06	017	23.8	23.8	0.0	0.0	2 610	1 250	1 360	08:50
23.06	018	29.2	29.2	0.0	0.0	1 450	1 390	60	07:45
24.06	019	19.0	19.0	0.0	0.0	2 200	2 090	110	10:30
25.06	020	17.0	17.0	0.0	0.0	1 590	1 660	-70	11:00
26.06	021	16.0	16.0	0.0	0.0	1 650	1 520	130	09:45
27.06									
28.06	022	16.5	16.5	0.0	0.0	1 260	1 020	240	04:50
29.06	023	10.9	10.9	0.0	0.0	1 560	590	970	06:00
30.06	024	12.9	12.9	0.0	0.0	1 210	1 610	-400	06:50
01.07	025	14.1	14.1	0.0	0.0	900	1 700	-800	06:30
02.07	026	6.9	6.9	0.0	0.0	810	150	660	03:10
03.07	027	12.9	12.9	0.0	0.0	1 230	1 890	-660	08:40
04.07	028	17.8	17.8	0.0	0.0	2 020	1 670	350	08:10
05.07	029	13.7	13.7	0.0	0.0	1 890	1 180	710	10:00
06.07	030	5.0	5.0	0.0	0.0	0	850	-850	01:40
07.07	031	11.5	11.5	0.0	0.0	950	230	720	06:00
08.07	032	17.0	17.0	0.0	0.0	1 390	1 260	130	08:30
09.07	033	18.9	18.9	0.0	0.0	530	2 240	-1 710	08:30
10.07	034	7.8	7.8	0.0	0.0	370	370	0	02:10

20.06.2015	49.0 km
03.08.2016	41.9 km
Total	
20.06.2016	84.3 km (b + k)

11.07	035	13.1	13.1	0.0	0.0	1 850	1 850	0	14:00
12.07	036	11.5	11.5	0.0	0.0	800	800	0	04:00
13.07	037	9.9	9.9	0.0	0.0	1 180	1 420	-240	07:00
14.07	038	10.8	10.8	0.0	0.0	1 440	470	970	07:20
15.07	039	10.4	10.4	0.0	0.0	400	2 070	-1 670	07:10
16.07	040	18.2	18.2	0.0	0.0	1 220	1 010	210	10:30
17.07									
18.07	041	7.9	7.9	0.0	0.0	690	60	630	02:55
19.07	042	9.0	9.0	0.0	0.0	1 700	2 180	-480	12:00
20.07	043	24.5	24.5	0.0	0.0	820	2 300	-1 480	08:30
21.07	044	22.4	22.4	0.0	0.0	2 340	1 490	850	10:20
22.07	045	14.6	14.6	0.0	0.0	520	1 600	-1 080	05:15
23.07	046	27.5	27.5	0.0	0.0	1 730	1 230	500	08:15
24.07	047	25.0	25.0	0.0	0.0	2 160	2 090	70	14:00
25.07	048	2.3	2.3	0.0	0.0	0	310	-310	00:25
26.07	049	2.3	2.3	0.0	0.0	310	0	310	00:40
27.07	050	19.7	19.7	0.0	0.0	1 570	1 800	-230	10:20
28.07	051	13.0	13.0	0.0	0.0	990	1 190	-200	07:30
29.07	052	9.4	9.4	0.0	0.0	420	890	-470	03:00
30.07	053	21.2	21.2	0.0	0.0	1 480	1 140	340	08:15
31.07	054	18.6	18.6	0.0	0.0	1 190	2 250	-1 060	07:00
01.08									

Summary: alone or not

114 days on the move

68 with others, of which

32 with a guide

18 with Peter

18 with other people

46 days alone

25.07.2015 not counted

02.08	055	20.0	20.0	0.0	0.0	1 690	2 390	-700	09:20
03.08	056	14.8	9.4	0.0	5.4	1 420	320	1 100	04:30
04.08	057	27.5	27.5	0.0	0.0	1 320	2 220	-900	07:40
05.08	058	17.8	9.4	0.0	8.4	110	230	-120	03:30
06.08	059	35.4	35.4	0.0	0.0	1 360	1 400	-40	09:00
07.08	060	28.5	28.5	0.0	0.0	1 700	1 210	490	07:30
08.08	061	29.8	27.5	0.0	2.3	1 110	1 560	-450	06:50
09.08	062	3.6	3.6	0.0	0.0	510	10	500	01:00
10.08	063	41.9	41.9	0.0	0.0	2 740	1 780	960	11:00
11.08	064	14.2	14.2	0.0	0.0	1 380	940	440	06:30
12.08	065	16.2	16.2	0.0	0.0	1 020	1 950	-930	08:10
13.08	066	14.2	14.2	0.0	0.0	1 100	2 030	-930	06:00
14.08	067	22.0	22.0	0.0	0.0	1 140	1 710	-570	06:40
15.08									
16.08	068	18.8	18.8	0.0	0.0	2 620	900	1 720	08:00
17.08	069	3.2	3.2	0.0	0.0	280	280	0	01:30
18.08	070	5.2	5.2	0.0	0.0	210	210	0	03:00
30.08	071	22.1	22.1	0.0	0.0	2 220	1 580	640	08:30
31.08	072	20.2	20.2	0.0	0.0	2 010	1 530	480	10:15
01.09	073	14.4	14.4	0.0	0.0	900	1 680	-780	05:50
02.09									

03.09									
04.09	074	23.6	23.6	0.0	0.0	1 510	1 730	-220	06:20
05.09	075	14.4	14.4	0.0	0.0	1 190	1 190	0	05:15
06.09	076	9.2	9.2	0.0	0.0	730	730	0	03:30
07.09									
01.10	077	6.0	6.0	0.0	0.0	270	160	110	01:30
02.10	078	16.4	16.4	0.0	0.0	1 260	1 260	0	06:30
03.10	079	18.7	18.7	0.0	0.0	1 180	1 290	-110	07:30
04.10	080	3.6	3.6	0.0	0.0	380	380	0	01:20
11.10	081	24.3	24.3	0.0	0.0	1 760	1 690	70	08:00
12.10	082	22.2	18.2	0.0	4.0	200	40	160	04:10
13.10	083	17.5	17.5	0.0	0.0	1 210	410	800	04:40
22.10	084	14.2	14.2	0.0	0.0	850	1 820	-970	10:45
23.10	085	15.1	15.1	0.0	0.0	530	1 150	-620	06:15
24.10	086	15.0	15.0	0.0	0.0	1 280	1 530	-250	06:55
02.11	087	19.3	19.3	0.0	0.0	1 850	1 570	280	08:30
03.11	088	25.4	25.4	0.0	0.0	1 160	1 480	-320	07:40
04.11	089	12.6	12.6	0.0	0.0	960	960	0	04:40

05.11	090	19.0	0.0	19.0	0.0	580	100	480	01:55
06.11	091	18.9	18.9	0.0	0.0	1 230	1 740	-510	06:10
07.11	092	27.9	27.9	0.0	0.0	1 310	1 680	-370	07:40
2016									
20.06	093	84.3	0.0	56.5	27.8	0	85	-85	07:35
21.06	094	48.6	0.0	31.2	17.4	95	100	-5	05:25
22.06	095	34.1	34.1	0.0	0.0	655	675	-20	07:30
23.06	096	73.1	0.0	73.1	0.0	1 220	1 160	60	06:45
24.06	097	51.3	0.0	51.3	0.0	595	685	-90	04:30
28.06	098	8.2	8.2	0.0	0.0	530	30	500	01:55
29.06	099	13.5	13.5	0.0	0.0	990	990	0	04:50
30.06	100	7.9	7.9	0.0	0.0	710	550	160	02:05
01.07	101	9.4	9.4	0.0	0.0	1 010	820	190	04:45
02.07	102	13.5	13.5	0.0	0.0	1 080	1 180	-100	05:40
03.07	103	12.2	12.2	0.0	0.0	1 310	1 310	0	08:40
04.07	104	16.7	16.7	0.0	0.0	1 120	1 810	-690	07:05
05.07									
06.07	105	22.3	22.3	0.0	0.0	1 610	1 610	0	06:55
07.07	106	24.9	24.9	0.0	0.0	1 750	1 750	0	07:55
08.07	107	24.4	24.4	0.0	0.0	1 945	1 835	110	07:35

09.07	108	27.0	27.0	0.0	0.0	450	690	-240	06:45
10.07	109	14.3	14.3	0.0	0.0	1 120	1 170	-50	05:10
11.07	110	14.0	14.0	0.0	0.0	1 100	900	200	04:50
12.07	111	17.5	17.5	0.0	0.0	170	1 580	-1 410	04:30
27.07	112	45.3	0.0	45.3	0.0	620	630	-10	05:00
03.08	113	41.9	0.0	0.0	41.9	0	30	-30	05:00
04.08	114	44.2	0.0	27.7	16.5	50	90	-40	03:50
06.08	115	27.4	27.4	0.0	0.0	660	680	-20	06:10

List of summits and important Alpine cols

(All heights and names have been as far as possible taken from the site map.geo.admin.ch 1:25'000 scale on-line maps. These are often not quite the same as those on the printed maps available for purchase.)

Date	Name	Height (m)		
2015				
06.06	Remelspitz	831		1
	Flühberg	787		2
	Roc au Corbeau	749		3
12.06	Le Meix Musy	1288		4
15.06	Grand Crêt	1419		5
22.06	Les Cornettes de Bise	2431		6
	Col de Verne	1813		
	Col d'Outanne	1856		
	Col de Recon	1734		
23.06	Haut Sé	1961		7
	Le Mouet	1936		8
	Pointe des Ombrieux	1981		9
	Cheval Blanc	1793		10
24.06	Col de Bossetan	2287		
	Pointe de la Golette	2634		11
	Dent de Barme	2759		12
25.06	Col du Sagerou	2394		
	Tête des Ottans	2548		13
	Col des Ottans	2498		
	Mont Ruan	3044		14
	Pointe des Rosses	2965	*	15
26.06	Col de Tanneverge	2484		
	Le Cheval Blanc	2830		16
28.06	Aiguillette	2321		17
	Col de Balme	2190	*	
29.06	Les Grandes Otanes	2679		18
	Pointe des Grands	310o	*	19
	Aiguilles du Pissoir	3439	*	20
	Aiguilles du Tour	3541		21

30.06	Fenêtre de Saleinaz	3261		
	Col du Chardonnet	3320		
	Aiguille d'Argentière	3898		22
01.07	Col du Tour Noir	3533		
03.07	Mont Dolent	3820		23
	Petit Col Ferret	2486		
	Grand Col Ferret	2536		
04.07	Grand Golliat, East summit	ca. 3150	*	24
	Col des Angroniettes	2935		
	Mont Fourchon	2901		25
	Fenêtre de Ferret	2695		
	Pointe de Drône	2949		26
	Grande Chenalette	2889		25
05.07	Col d'Annibal	2990		
	Mont Vélan	3722		28
07.07	Col d'Otemma	3209		
08.07	Col de l'Evêque	3379		
	Col de Collon	3068	*	
09.07	Tête Blanche	3710	*	29
11.07	Colle del Leone	3578		
	Pic Tyndall	4239		30
	Mont Cervin – Matterhorn	4477		31
12.07	Testa Grigia	3479		
13.07	Breithornpass	3813	*	
12.07	Breithorn	4164		32
13.07	Pollux	4092		33
	Zwillingsjoch	3846		
	Castor	4223		34
	Felikjoch	4063		
14.07	Lisjoch	4152		
	Ludwigshöhe	4342		35
	Parrotspitze	4434		36
	Signalkuppe – Punta Gnifetti (Capanna Regina Margherita CAI)	4553		37
15.07	Zumsteinspitze	4562		38
	Grenzgipfel	4617	*	39
	Dunantspitze	4632		40
	Dufourspitze	4634		41
	Silbersattel	4519		
	Nordend	4608		42
16.07	Cima di Jazzi	3796		43

18.07	Monte Moropass	2852		
19.07	Joderhorn	3035		44
	Mondellipass	2830		
	Pizzo Mondelli	2958		45
	Spechhorn – Pizzo di Antigine	3188		46
	Ofentalhorn	3059		47
	Ofentalpass	2833		
	Jazzihorn – Pizzo Cingino Nord	3226		48
	Antronapass	2837		
	Passo Camposecco	3137		
	Vorder Latelhorn	3192		49
20.07	Passo d'Andolla	2409		
21.07	Monte Leone	3554		50
22.07	Chaltwasserpass	2770		
22.07	Wasenhorn – Punta Terrarossa	3246		51
23.07	Albrunpass	2407		
24.07	Eggerscharte	2856		
	Ofenhorn – Punta d'Arbola	3236		52
	Hohsandjoch	2899	*	
	Ober Hohsandjoch	3005		
	Hohsandhorn – Punta del Sabbione	3181		53
	Blinnenhorn – Corno Cieco	3374		54
	Rothornpass – Gran Sella del Gries	3091		
	Griespass	2451		
27.07	Passo San Giacomo	2306		
	Bocchetta di Val Maggia	2633		
	Basòdino	3272		55
	Passo d'Antabia	3033		
28.07	Passo Cazzòla	2411		
	Pizzo Cazzòla	2756		56
30.07	Pilone – Cima Pian del Bozzo	2192		57
02.08	Testa di Misello	1596		58
	Rocce del Gridone	2155		59
	Bocchetta del Fornale	2033		
	Gridone – Monte Limidario	2186		60
03.08	Monte Paglione – Paión	1554		61
04.08	Monte Lema	1619		62
06.08	Poncione d'Arzo	1017		63
07.08	Passo Bonello	1105		
08.08	Monte Generoso – Calvagione	1700		64
	Cima della Piancaccia	1610		65

	Cima dei Torrioni	1488		66
10.08	Denti della Vecchia	1490	*	67
	Cima Mosè	1726		68
	Cima di Fojorina	1809		69
	Bocchetta di San Bernardo	1585		
	Monte Cucco – Dosso Colmine	1623		70
	Passo di San Lucio	1540		
	Gazzirola	2115		71
	Monte Segor	2096		72
	Monte Stabiello	2114		73
	Mottone della Tappa	2130		74
	Bocchetta di Sommafiume	1924		
	Passo San Jorio	2011		
11.08	Cima di Cugn	2237		75
	Bocchetta di Stazzona	2121		
	Bocchetta di Camedo	1970		
12.08	Bocchetta del Notar	2095		
13.08	Pizzo Tambo	3279		76
	Splügenpass – Passo dello Spluga	2114		
14.08	Pass da Niemet	2281		
16.08	Bocchetta della Tegiola	2489		
31.08	Cima di Castello	3379		77
01.09	Sella del Forno	2769		
	Monte del Forno	3213		78
	Passo del Muretto	2559		
05.09	Pass da Canfinal	2625		
03.09	Col d'Anzana	2220		
02.09	pt 2647 (Monte Masuccio)	2647		
	Pass Portun	2631		
04.09	Bocchetta di Braga	2569		
	L'Om	2787		79
	Pass da l'Om	2747		
02.10	Pass da Sach	2731		
	Frontier stone no. 11, near Pass da Val Viola	2431		
03.10	Pass da Val Mera	2670		
	Piz Ursera	3031		80
	Forcola di Livigno	2314		
04.10	La Stretta	2465		
11.10	Piz La Stretta – Monte Breva	3103		81
	Monte Garone	3029		82

		Fuorcla Federia	2899	
13.10		Pass Umbrail	2501	
22.10		Piz da las Trais Linguas	2843	83
		Sella da Piz Cotschen	2922	
		Korspitz	2932	84
		Klein Tartscher Kopf – Cima Piccola di Tàrres	2917	85
		Fuorcla Costainas	2804	
		Furkelspitz – Piz Costainas	3003	86
24.10		La Scharta	2592	
		Piz Chavalatsch	2762	87
02.11		Piz Terza – Urtirolaspitz	2908	88
		Fuorcla Starlex	2629	
03.11		Schlinigpass – Passo di Slìngia	2297	
		Rasasserscharte	2716	
04.11		Grubenjoch – Giogo delle Fosse	2645	
		Piz Lad	2807	89
06.11		Grübelekopf	2892	90
		Flimjoch	2756	
07.11		Zeblasjoch	2538	
		Fuorcla Val Gronda	2750	
2016				
29.06		Kronenjoch	2974	
		Bischofspitze	3028	91
		Grenzeckkopf – Piz Faschalba	3047	92
		Pass Futschöl	2767	
01.07		Dreiländerspitz	3196	93
		Vermuntpass – Fuorcla Vermunt	2796	
02.07		Grosser Piz Buin – Piz Buin Grond	3312	94
		Fuorcla dal Cunfin	3041	
03.07		Signalhorn	3207	95
		Egghorn	3147	96
		Silvrettahorn	3243	97
		Rotflue	3165	98
		Rote Furka	2686	
04.07		Plattenjoch	2727	
06.07		Carnäirajoch	2488	
		Hinterberg	2681	99
		Schlappiner Joch	2201	

07.07	Gafier Joch	2406		
08.07	St. Antönier Joch – Gargällerjoch	2376		
	Riedchopf – Ronggspitz	2551		100
	Plasseggenpass	2351		
	Gruobenpass	2229		
	Sulzfluh	2817		101
09.07	Schweizertor	2137		
10.07	Gamsluggen	2374		
	Schesaplana	2965		102
11.07	Gross Furgga – Hochjoch	2358		
	Naafkopf	2569		103

*Summit or col not actually stood on, but very close, at a stone's throw, less than a minute away (vegetation, other people, wind, etc.)

Acknowledgements

The whole adventure would not have been possible without the help and support of the many people listed below.

I am especially grateful to my wife Sally for her unwavering encouragement, also for driving me to remote places, not always on good roads. My thanks also to family members who helped me in one way or another and/or accompanied me on several sections: our son Roger for loan of equipment, driving to the other end of the country at least three times and accompanying me on several sections; grandsons Natan and Neil for helping me along Lake Geneva, Neil Cointet also for his role as photographer the first few days on the western border of Switzerland, as well as logistical help and for hiking with me; daughters Sonia and Natalie, grandchildren Leo and Tessa Farrell for their company, in the Silvretta and for the last few kilometres in Basel respectively.

My sincere thanks to Fritz and Ursulina Hagmann for help and advice during difficult periods in the Grisons (Fritz notably "rescued" me from the hospital in Sondalo), Nona Rowat for her presence and logistical help in Ticino, Yves Stettler for ferrying me and guide Dave Green from above Bourg St-Pierre to the Val de Bagnes and organising the onward trip to the Chanrion mountain hut, François Chastellain for the very idea of the "Frontier Stories" and for checking my French compositions.

Others who accompanied me for one or more days: Christoph Brändle, Walter Roschnik, Peter Rowat, Urs Scholer and Yves Stettler.

The eight guides who led me competently for one or more days: Victor Sanders, Graham Frost, Dave Green, Euan Whittaker, Dave Kenyon, Giorgio Cazzanelli, Lukas Mathis and David Hefti. Special thanks to Graham's wife Janine who did much of the work finding and hiring the first five of these.

And not least, all those who followed my progress on my website and many of whom encouraged me by posting messages on my website, too numerous to mention, which helped me maintain morale.

* * *

Photo credits

This book contains one or more pictures by Christoph Brändle, Neil Cointet, Graham Frost, David Hefti, Roger Roschnik, Sally Roschnik, Sonia Roschnik, Walter Roschnik, Nona Rowat, Peter Rowat and Euan Whittaker, who made their work available to me. My thanks to all of them!

The large maps near the beginning of each main chapter are based on a physical topographical map of Switzerland in Wikimedia Commons, © Tschubby, CCA 2.5 Generic.

Photo of the Splügen pass road: Wikimedia Commons, © Adrian Michael, CCA 2.5 Generic.

Photo of Achilles platter: Ex flickr, © Carole Raddato.

Two smaller maps are included with the permission of the Swiss Federal Office of Topography (swisstopo). They are taken from the site map.geo.admin.ch whose maps are excellent and extremely valuable for planning excursions.

Further details on my website www.swiss-perimeter.ch